SOUL
NEVER
SLEEPS

Advanced Perceptions
to a More Loving, Purposeful,
and Joyous Life

By
Marian Massie, CL.H.

Advanced
Perceptions, Inc.

1820 Water Place
Suite 150
Atlanta, Georgia 30339
404-956-0554

SOUL NEVER SLEEPS
Advanced Perceptions to a
More Loving, Purposeful, and Joyous Life

© 1992 by Marian Massie

The spiritual teachings mentioned in this text are those derived from the author's personal experience and do not represent the official positions of Eckankar or Buddhism. The intent of the author is only to offer information of a general nature to help you on your quest for spiritual, mental, emotional, and physical growth. In the event you may use any of the information in this book for yourself, which is your constitutional right, the author and the publisher assume no responsibility for your actions.

Library of Congress Catalog Number 92-72272
ISBN 0-9633140-2-5

Cover Art: © 1991 by Marian Massie
Book and Cover Design: Couch Communications, Atlanta, GA
Editor: Phyllis Mueller, Atlanta GA
Author's Photo: Dan Brogdon, Atlanta GA

Published and distributed in the United States by:

Advanced Perceptions Inc.
1820 Water Place
Suite 150
Atlanta, Georgia 30339

Printed in the United States of America

I dedicate
this book
to all
as a gift
of love!

May the
blessings
be!

In Appreciation

I want to acknowledge several people who have been and are very dear in my life:

No one could have a better, more loving friend than my great friend Beth. She has always been there for me and listened to me. Her openness and support have been invaluable.

My sister Judith has helped me appreciate art and the creative process. I want to thank my sister Jean for always accepting me just the way I am. And Gail and Joan, I deeply appreciate your encouragement for this project.

I thank Greg for helping me believe in myself and listening to me when I needed to talk.

I greatly appreciate the guidance and abilities of Phyllis. Without her help, this book may never have manifested.

And I especially thank Paul, who came into my life to help me open my heart more fully to love. Through knowing him, I have grown tremendously.

I also want to thank all my clients. Knowing them has helped me to learn and grow.

CONTENTS

Exercises in Growth and Healing

Throughout this book, you will find many kinds of exercises to help you grow in mind, body and Spirit. Feel free to use them alone or in combination with others. This is a quick reference of the different exercises you will find in each chapter.

Advanced Perceptions

We have choices to make
in this life of ours.
How do we want to live?
How do we truly want to be,
or to see,
this life of ours?

Each day's actions
are a declaration
of advancement, independence, and awareness;
or retreat, victimhood, and darkness.

This moment
is precious you see.
For in this now
links you with eternity.

Your eternal nows are
creating your life, your awareness,
your perceptions,
of what is real and true
for you.

And we all have the power of choice;
Accumulated creates
your life,
your you,
your now.

The courageous march forward.
Ever wanting the new ways.
The advanced perception!
Of life, of living, of being.

Introduction

This book is a culmination of my lifelong inner growth and professional observations with thousands of clients. Mankind is at a crossroads of development: we can now destroy ourselves or evolve in our awareness of what we truly are meant to become. This book is not just about changing your beliefs, healing your inner child, or overcoming problems. This book is really about changing your perspective of life and your awareness of who you are and the reality of life as you have known it. Yes, we need to heal our inner children and overcome our dysfunctional childhoods but, more importantly, while we heal and grow the emotional or mental parts of ourselves, we need to remember the real reason we are here at all.

My book helps to integrate and heal every level of your being, while helping you awaken to the fact that your truest self is Soul. Living with this advanced perception helps you with any issues in your daily life and assists you in going beyond the mundane to the sublime! I want this book to be a guide for you and a catalyst for your future exploration of life and reality. Only when we live with the realization that we are indeed spiritual beings who are here to learn and grow from this earthly experience, can we live our lives fully.

It is a truly remarkable experience how this book even came into existence. In 1987 I had a dream. A very powerful dream. It was the kind of dream that made me sit up and take notice. This dream revealed to me that I was going to write two books to help people grow in spirit, joy, harmony, and happiness. This is the first!

I am a Clinical Hypnotherapist and I've had a successful private practice for over seven years. I personally use the principles in this book, and I also incorporate them during therapy to help my clients reach their objectives. Since these teachings continually work, I now want to share them with more people.

Whether you want to feel better about yourself or your life or you want to grow in consciousness, these teachings can help tremendously. I have incorporated my life experiences, not just theoretical knowledge, into my perspective as a therapist and with the teachings in this book. I have lived through most of the problems anyone could have, and I have grown as a person because of the way I chose to learn through my problems. My life used to be a lonely, empty experience; now my life is filled with joy, harmony, balance, creativity, and love. And I find these positive aspects increasing in my life more each day.

I'm writing this book from my heart and Soul; I never before have been a professional writer. I hope this book can help other Souls grow in Spirit, get closer to God and lead happier and more purposeful lives. For this is the purpose of this book: to help you become the best person you can be, and help you manifest your highest, happiest self in this lifetime.

This book has been guided by what I call Spirit and my higher self, or Soul. Even though I have always been afraid of writing, my powerful dream experiences guided and encouraged me, step by step, all the way. These two reasons show me that God does indeed have a sense of humor. What better and more profound way to teach others that they can accomplish seemingly impossible goals and overcome their limitations, than by inspiring someone who can't spell and who hates to write and compel her to write a book? So for me to author a book is like asking a person with crutches to go for a 10-mile run, uphill!

4

But somewhere in my Soul, I knew this book would manifest someday. I have always relied on my intuition, because it has been so accurate my whole life. I felt that someday I would write these books and when the time came, somehow I'd have the ability to do it. But I thought I'd write when I was old and grey with nothing else to do. Boy was I mistaken! One of the basic principles you will find in this book is the integration of Spirit into your daily life. This book is a manifestation of just this kind of integration. This integration or communication of Spirit comes through many forms such as your intuition or dreams.

After my profound dream, I did not run to a typewriter or to a computer. I did nothing for two years. I just remembered my dream and held onto my feeling of knowing that this book would manifest. I was not ready to move forward on this project, because I had inner work to accomplish first.

Then one night I heard my Soul. Through a second dream I was very vividly shown how to write this book. Then I was excited! I started writing the outline for this book in longhand, and I dislike writing in longhand more than I hate eating beets!

Then I quit writing for another year. In my heart I was terrified of this endeavor. About a year later, the urge to write emerged again, and this time it stayed. The feeling was so overwhelming that I could no longer deny what I needed to do. So, in essence, I have written the book of my dreams!

The information you will read here is not new. It has been taught for as long as mankind has been around. I am telling it in my own way, with my own words, from my own experiences.

I use these laws of life and truths in my own life and I teach them to my clients. I am not forcing anyone to hear or to believe what I say. Truth, Spirit, and love do not have to be shoved down anyone's throat. People grow when they are ready. You will change only when you want to and not before.

This book and the information contained within its pages are for individuals who are ready for a higher experience of what life is all about. I am writing for all the people who want to live this higher existence and awareness NOW! The teachings of this book are advanced perceptions of how to understand and live life.

In this book I have integrated many teachings, from the physical and therapeutic to the spiritual, with everything in between. The format of the chapters has a specific purpose. The poetry will reach a different part of you and the basic information still another. With this format I am hoping to reach the total person.

You learn on many different levels. You learn differently from prose, and poetry reaches your heart in places you didn't know you had. The basic chapters, though, are the foundation from which to work. I clearly saw in my dreams that the book was to have poetry with each chapter.

All the work in this book, from the poetry to the cover art, is mine. As with my writing, I have never before been a professional artist or poet. When you integrate your life with Spirit, you can accomplish anything! This whole creative endeavor is a testimony to the power of Spirit helping me in my life, and it can now help you. I firmly believe I couldn't have done this project without the integration of Spirit in my life.

If you want more from life, read on. You can read this book through, or you can study the individual chapters. You can read a particular chapter that pertains to your present circumstance regarding any situation in your life without reading the book in order. I hope this book can be a tool for you to be the captain of your own destiny and help you bring about a higher awareness into your daily life!

Responsibility

Oooooo—That horrid word.
What dark emotions it can evoke
Dank and musty,
the root rot of growth.
Seriousness,
Authorities impinging on our rights.
But wait,
Let's shed more light...
a greater depth of understanding,
of this responsibility.
See it growing and happy.
Strong with joy and direction.
The master of its own evolution!
Ah, what beautiful emotions it
evokes,
What a beautiful life
it can create! ❧

Chapter 1

Responsibility

All around us we see economic upheaval, governments in collapse, environmental decay, rising crime, disillusioned and disheartened people. Are we on the fast track to doom?

History bears witness to our struggle to find peace, happiness and joy. This struggle has been played out in a myriad of ways. The Industrial Revolution gave us tremendous mechanical capability, but there is still poverty, economic upheaval, and social unrest. Next we looked to science to find the answers to life through physical measuring, trying to verify our reality by quantifying it. All around us, we see enormous scientific advances in medicine and technology, but our increased knowledge has yet to solve our problems or elevate the human condition.

In the past fifty years, we have seen a vast emphasis on the material. Human consumption and demand for goods are at an all-time high. Having and wanting more have not given us lasting joy or peace. All around us we still see hatred, struggle for power, and wanton waste. Through our lack of awareness, we have even come to the brink of destroying our home, planet Earth.

We have grown in intellect through the ages, amassing knowledge on many subjects, yet we have grasped very little wisdom or inner peace about life. Philosophy, religion, and psychology have fallen short in helping us deal harmoniously and effectively with daily life. Still we have economic upheaval, poverty, and social unrest. Increased knowledge, as we have witnessed, has not solved our problems or elevated the human condition. Despair and chaos are more noticeable today because of the sheer numbers of people who intensify the situation.

Why have we not found the peace and lasting joy that we dearly seek? There are answers to our questions and problems, and the answers lie in the voluntary evolution of the consciousness of each individual. A new order and attention to life has to happen to reverse our downward spiral. To create the massive outer changes we all want, we first have to start living life from a more evolved, higher awareness. Through the individual tremendous changes in the whole structure of life on this planet can occur. As more and more individuals evolve and change, their evolution will affect the reality of the entire planet!

This book is a study of life and its different realities. It presents a very grounded approach for the individual who wants to reach that higher awareness and who is ready to live life with greater love, purpose and awareness. Its teachings and truths can benefit anyone, but only can be absorbed by a person who is ready to hear them, whose consciousness is open and ready to change and grow.

Knowing Truth ✌

Please use this book as a tool and a guide for your spiritual, emotional, and personal growth. The ultimate authority on what you need in your life or what is true in the universe has to come from within the depths of your own being. People and books can only help reveal the truth. Only you will know if something has value or is real for you because you KNOW it and not because someone has told you it is true. The reason I have this chapter first is because this whole book is based on your willingness to find out through your own experience if what I am saying is true or not. You can choose to take responsibility and actions with the teachings in this book, which will then help you know if what I am saying is true for you.

The knowing I am talking about goes beyond an intellectual understanding. It is the way you connect to yourself as an all-knowing, spiritual being. That connection may not be readily apparent every day, but when you get "feelings" or awareness of just knowing for no particular reason, then realize you have tapped into your higher self. Higher growth and awareness are achieved when you are your own authority. If you constantly do things, even good things, because others have told you to or because you feel you "should" or "ought to," you have relinquished your free will and you are then living your life no more consciously than a robot. Living life with full consciousness should be everyone's goal, because the more you live your life with this deep awareness, the more you connect to your higher self as Soul. The spiritual part of yourself as Soul is totally free. Living consciously is a part of this total freedom.

Now, I am not telling you to rebel against what other people have taught you just for the sake of rebelling. What I am saying is most of us have relinquished responsibility for our individual lives to others. Most of us have not let ourselves feel or test out these teachings to find out if they are creating value or if they can create positive change in our lives. Most people never ask if what they are being taught is something they want for themselves. They are in fact giving up personal responsibility when they do this. Living unaware or unconscious, in essence, is living as a robot.

True Responsibility ❧

The reason people live this way is because on some level they don't want to take responsibility for **ALL** of their life. Oh, most of us are willing to take care of the day-to-day stuff and most do the best possible job. We see to it the bills are paid and the house is clean and we go to work on time. We get caught up in daily routine and forget, or just don't realize responsibility on Earth is more than taking care of the human body and making it through the day. As a human being, your true purpose is to become aware of all aspects of yourself and live consciously with this awareness. This awareness includes your mind, body, emotions, and spirit. This is true responsibility!

Most people are not happy or content. They feel empty, without purpose, and do not know why. Yet most people don't want to explore the greater depths of life to search and find the answers to living. Society has lived with the quick fix or the "magic pill" philosophy for too long. Contentment and happiness can be achieved only when individuals awaken to their true purpose, connecting to their selves as Soul. Even if you have acquired great wealth, healed your inner child, and consistently think positively, there will still be an inner yearning to know why you were born and what happens after physical death.

Conducting therapy with thousands of people over the years, I have seen that most people willingly or unwillingly live as victims. Victims do not take full responsibility for their lives. They live as children, unconsciously ignorant of the laws that govern life, caught up in what they want when they want it, with no thought to the consequences of their actions. (As with children, it doesn't mean we're bad; it is just as yet we don't know any other way to be.)

I feel until people grasp the truth of life and *live* this truth daily, they are living less of a life when they are not consciously living each day, or at least trying to live, in union with Spirit, their highest self (Soul), and God.

People come to this deeper understanding of life either by life experience or by evolving through a spiritual practice. The vehicle for your higher awareness will always come into your life when you are sincerely seeking change and truth. There is an old saying: "The teacher or teaching arrives when the student is ready." I am a firm believer that when you are ready for this new awareness, you will be shown how to proceed.

What Is Life About? ðₐ

All of life and our individual experiences are here to help us get closer to God. The word "God," to some people, evokes fear, anger, distrust, and myriads of other emotions. Most of us have been raised with the beliefs that the creator of all existence, God, is a judgmental, rule-producing being and we should feel shamed and guilt-ridden for our very existence. I believe God is LOVE. Because God is love, *when we truly love ourselves, we in turn love and serve God.* As humans, throughout our history, we have limited our beliefs and understanding about God for various reasons. We have let our parents, scholars, and religious leaders interpret our understanding of God. Most of us have abdicated our individual responsibility of knowing about God to these "authorities." We must be our own spiritual authorities to grow and fully live this reality.

Choosing How to Live ðₐ

This life of yours is a lesson in awareness and self-love of the highest order. Your schoolroom is Mother Earth and the classes are your daily lives. Whether you are a housewife, an executive, a rocket scientist, or a prisoner, you have picked these roles to help you learn your lessons and evolve as the true you: Soul. Your lives are roles you have chosen, to teach you something you need to learn. Though each life is so very different, all are "perfect." We get exactly what we need to grow to our highest potential. What you get may not be what you want consciously for your material or emotional self, but your higher self or Soul knows what experiences you need in order to grow to attain your highest potential. Through your experiences you can grow and achieve awareness and union with God, if you choose to see the higher lessons contained within daily life.

So how does this pertain to responsibility? As a human being, you are given free will. Each moment, you can choose to live life with responsibility toward your higher good or to live and act as a victim. Victims live life from the belief (conscious or unconscious) that circumstances are out of their control, and that they have no power to change.

Life is a series of lessons to help you grow in love, freedom, and awareness. People who live from their higher nature, whether they are conscious of it or not, choose to learn from these lessons or problems. The victims of the world do not. You are given the right to live in darkness and ignorance or to use all of your energy to get closer to God and Spirit, which is the totality of love, freedom, and bliss. This, in fact, is your **true** purpose for your being alive.

So this may bring you to ask the questions: Why are some of us living in a free country while others are prisoners or starving in other parts of the world? Why are some people born healthy and others born with defects? Why is it that when you try to live life with Spirit and God, sometimes your life seems to get worse?

Well, to answer those questions brings us to discuss two very important laws of life. Some of you might not agree with these laws, and that's okay. All I ask of anyone, whether the person is in therapy with me or reading this book, is that you give yourself permission to be open to hearing teachings that may be new to you. Then go within yourself and find out if what I say, or what anything anyone else has to say for that matter, helps you create value for your life right now. Read this book with your "heart" as well as with your mind, and try to keep both as open as possible.

I also want to point out that when you choose to be on the road to a higher awareness in your life, a teaching may be correct for you for a minute, a day, or a lifetime. You will know when a teaching is correct for you if it creates value in your life. It brings you closer to "being" love. A correct teaching will help you become more independent and self-reliant. You will know if a teaching is right for you when it helps you become more balanced, happy, and aware of your true self as Soul. A true teaching helps open your heart fully to love and Spirit, which is really what life is all about.

As your consciousness grows and changes, what helped you before may no longer be right. For example, what worked for you in the second grade may no longer work for you in college.

What you hopefully will understand from this book is growth, reality, and truth are ever-changing. There are laws and teachings that are constant, true, and correct for you at all stages of your growth, and there are some you will want to discard as your awareness of life grows. As you develop inner wisdom and self-discernment, you will know what is valuable for your life in the present moment. You must control your own life. Only you can know what is necessary for your next growth step. If at times you are unsure, you will gain wisdom only by doing for yourself. Nobody can live your life for you. No one can tell you what is inside your heart or what you may need next for your unfoldment as an individual or as truest self—Soul.

So the two principles I will discuss now, in conjunction with responsibility, are Cause and Effect, and Reincarnation. It would be difficult to understand how to live with total responsibility without understanding these two principles.

15

Cause and Effect and Reincarnation ❧

Cause and Effect, simply stated, means that for whatever action you take in your life, you will receive a condition or result because of that action. Actions are thoughts, words, or physical deeds; they can be positive or negative. The more positive actions you make, the more positive your life becomes. Negative actions create negative results. Positive actions create value for you and all of life; negative actions devalue you or life in some way. Cause and Effect governs this plane of existence, just as gravity is still present and working in this physical dimension whether you are aware of it or not. The more you live your life consciously, aware of Cause and Effect, the more control you will have to create your life the way you want it to be, while at the same time creating value for the whole of life.

Reincarnation means each Soul is born into a plane of existence to learn the lessons it needs to know to grow in its awareness and union with God. The individual Soul needs more than one lifetime of experience. This is because there is so much to learn about the aspects of Spirit, Itself and God.

Cause and Effect and Reincarnation are very closely tied together. The actions you make are influencing and creating your future. The moment called "now" literally creates your future in this life as well as influencing the next. What actions you have made in the past (in this lifetime or another) affected your present.

Cause and Effect and Reincarnation very clearly explain why some people are born handicapped and some people are not. They explain why some people are born in countries that control freedom and why some are born in countries which uphold the individual's rights. Apparent discrepancies in life are the result of previous actions in

16

other lifetimes. The results surface as accumulated positive or negative effects, or "karma." Karma, a word of Buddhist and Hindu origin, is a name for the results of all the actions we have ever made from the very beginning of our existence.

Karma ॐ

A person will receive what is right and deserving, though a person may not necessarily get back the specific effect from someone or something in the past. Karma is exacting; in other words, people receive what they deserve, based on their past actions. For example, your control of another person in a former life could come back to you as the "same" person you controlled now controlling you in this life. Or the same lesson could surface as a new person or circumstance controlling you. Your lessons can take a hundred scenarios, but the essence of the lesson would be exact. This is how I interpret karma.

Remember, karma can be positive or negative, depending on your actions. An example of positive karma can be something good happening in this life, like being born in a free country or into a wealthy family. Negative karma could be a child born with a defect. With these examples, somewhere in the past, positive and negative effects were accumulated and the results are manifesting in this lifetime.

All your experiences and karma can help bring about your enlightenment. The more you view life not as a series of problems but as a series of learning experiences, the faster and more spiritually evolved you become.

Life is eternal, and it may take awhile for your negative karma to catch up with you. This is the reason why many people seem to "get away with murder." (They really don't; it just seems that way because of the lag in time for repayment.) Effects from a former life may not manifest until this lifetime or another. By the time the results of your past actions manifest, you won't remember why they are happening. You don't remember that maybe in the past you weren't all that kind or glorious a person. We all have done things in former lives we would be ashamed of in this life. We also have done many wonderful and loving things. Just remember—whatever is manifesting in your life or mine, you and I have made the actions to create these experiences, good or bad. This is true whether you remember what you did to create these circumstances or not.

You, as Soul, need all kinds of experiences to grow in knowing God. We all have free will to make choices in each moment. No matter what your past was like or what you may have done, what really counts is the moment, the ever-present "now." It is only in the "now" that you have the power to change. The more you live your daily life with awareness of the incredible power in each of your moments and align your consciousness and actions with Spirit and God, the higher and faster you will evolve. You can dispel negative karma in the present moment only and it is done by aligning your actions to the highest purpose of life. As you consciously increase and use this understanding, you become more attuned to the higher aspects of life. At the same time, you create a more positive future for yourself.

My Story 🍂

Now let me tell you how I came to believe in this way of thinking and how these beliefs have affected my own life. I come from an upper middle-class family. My father owned his own business and I am the youngest of eight (yes, count 'em, eight) children. Needless to say, my parents were Catholics and we were all raised strictly Catholic.

Please understand, I am NOT preaching for or against any belief or faith. I firmly believe whatever path or religion you are practicing is perfect for you now. If you are not practicing any formal religion or belief, that's also perfect for you now.

If you choose to relinquish a certain belief, that doesn't make your former belief bad or wrong. It just makes it not right for you now. In my own personal road to growth and awareness I have practiced and tried different religions and beliefs. These have been good for me and my awareness in the time I held them. And when I lived my life with no formal religion and just observed life, that too was perfect and invaluable. All those experiences helped me grow. Life is your teacher. All of life's answers are within yourself. Every experience is your teacher, when you let the teaching into your awareness.

Early Childhood ❧

I grew up in what is now called a dysfunctional home, though at the time none of us knew a name for it. I always thought something was strange and off-kilter in the way my family related, because no one in my family talked about feelings. I always felt alone with my own thoughts and feelings, with no one ever to talk to.

My world and my family's world evolved around my mother's constant sickness. From my first remembrances until her death when I was 23, I never saw her well or happy. She had breast cancer when I was just five. At that time, the treatment for breast cancer was extremely brutal. Her chest was totally scarred from the operations and she had no breasts or nipples. She also had to have intense radiation treatments. The radiation left her skin red and raw and her energy totally drained. The amounts of radiation she received would never be given now.

Over my childhood, my mother was in and out of hospitals almost every year. She had one kidney removed, her thyroid out, a hysterectomy, and all her teeth taken out. Needless to say, she was always in pain. Because of the intense pain from the cancer, her doctors prescribed morphine, and she became addicted. I remember one night—I think it was around dinner time—when she started to go into convulsions. I was very young and truly petrified by what I witnessed. My mother started gagging on her own tongue and she was unaware of what was happening to her. Everyone was racing around trying to help and I was sent to my room. I remember my sister Judy telling me to pray for her. I thought my mother was going to die, but she didn't. This was just another "normal" occurrence in our household. This kind of drama was always being played out in our house.

That event was traumatic for any child, but no one in our house talked to me about my mother's illness. We never discussed the traumas or problems our family experienced. When I look back on my childhood, the thing I remember the most was being terribly lonely. I felt lonely because there was no one for me to talk over my thoughts with and no one to listen to me. I had no emotional connection to anyone. I especially felt the loss of not being listened to, because I was the "baby" of the family, and who listens to the youngest child? Ironic, isn't it? I come from a family of eight children, ten people including the adults, and I felt lonely *all* the time. This lack of communication is very normal for dysfunctional families.

Dysfunctional Families ❧

People in dysfunctional families are taught directly and indirectly not to communicate their deep feelings and to lock those feelings away and not let them surface. You are taught to bury your head in the sand, to deny your reality because reality is too scary. So it becomes easy to deny the truth of your pain. What is truly crazy or unbalanced in a dysfunctional home life is thought to be "normal." As John Bradshaw teaches so well in his book *Healing the Shame that Binds You*, you are taught consciously or unconsciously to view yourself as a mistake. When individuals come from dysfunctional backgrounds, the children haven't gotten the message from their upbringing they were loved UNCONDITIONALLY. They did not get the proper nurturing so they, in turn, could learn to love themselves. Little children need love and a healthy self-esteem mirrored back to them from their environment, which includes the parents and other members of their family, in order to feel love and self-worth. Children in dysfunctional homes have been brought up to nurture their parents and deny their own feelings. This lack of positive, healthy mirroring creates shame and feelings of worthlessness. These feelings stay inside the little child who then becomes the wounded adult, until these feelings are faced and processed healthily. Some ways in which you can help yourself process your feelings healthily are explained later in greater detail.

The majority of us, if not all of us, come from some kind of a dysfunctional home. A dysfunctional home can be a household of little or no emotional involvement, sexual abuse, heavy criticism, drug and/or alcohol abuse, physical and/or emotional abandonment, or tremendous sickness, like in my family. What characterizes a dysfunctional home is **any** kind of environment that creates in a person a conscious, or more correctly an unconscious, feeling of self-hate, worthlessness, or guilt, just for being. The dysfunctional person sees himself or herself as "less than" and different than other people. You may feel like you don't belong anywhere or you may feel like a mistake.

Unknowingly I grew up hating myself and feeling

totally worthless. I felt isolated and different from other people. Unconsciously, I was terribly angry at my mother for not nurturing me, and I felt tremendous guilt for being so angry at her. It was a perpetuating cycle of self-hate. I never realized any of these feelings consciously until I was in my mid-twenties.

Most of the clients I see come from dysfunctional homes. And most of the people coming from these situations don't understand their feelings or why they make the choices they make. What happens is that all the negative unconscious beliefs created from their childhood affect their daily lives now. They are constantly carrying in their hearts all the hurt and neglect from their upbringing.

My Mom and Dad ?♠

In my upbringing, my mother not only was sick all the time, but she also was addicted to valium and alcohol. I remember times I'd come home from school and she'd be upstairs and I'd be downstairs and I'd hear a "thud." The thud was her falling to the floor; the valium and alcohol had affected her balance.

My mother couldn't emotionally be there for me or anyone else in my family. I know she loved me and she was a good person, but this didn't change the realities of our family life and what was missing in my upbringing as a child. As a child my emotional self never got the love or nurturing I so dearly needed to grow to be a fully-functioning, healthy adult.

My brother Mike and I were most affected by her incapacitation because we were the last of the children living at home. When I was in elementary school, my other brothers and sisters were out of the house and my father was absorbed in his business. When he'd come home at night, usually very late, he would retreat, read his business magazines, or go to bed. I don't ever remember him asking me what I did in school that day or if I had any problems. I never remember him listening or relating to me on the emotional level I needed.

Everyone outside the family loved him. To them he was a real outgoing guy, always very positive and enthusiastic. He was definitely enthusiastic, the opposite of my mother. My mother was negative, unhappy, and physically weak. My father looked 20 years younger than his actual age and was very healthy, strong, and always tried to be positive. As positive as he appeared, he never showed his heart to me. Though I loved my father, I could never communicate deeply with him and I never felt him try to connect to me as a person. I could not imagine going to him when I was a child, crying and hurt, and him being there for me with tenderness or warmth and making my hurt all better. We got the message in our family we had to be strong and perfect. Your emotions, if not happy or positive, were a sign of weakness.

My father's extreme positiveness and my mother's negativeness were both examples of dysfunctional behavior. My father's dysfunctional behavior was harder to spot, because he hid his real feelings beneath his positive veneer. Both my parents denied their full spectrum of feelings. Consequentially, this behavior was learned by their children.

I chose to emulate my father's behavior because, outwardly, he looked like a survivor. All I saw in my mother's life was pain, misery, and death. The choice, albeit unconscious, was easy for me: life or death. I chose what I perceived was life. In choosing my father's way of dealing with life, I stuffed all anger, sadness, and loneliness deep inside myself. I would allow myself only to be strong and show strength. And the only way I could communicate to others was on a superficial level. I wore the perpetual "happy face" for society, but I was dying inside!

In my home I was designated as the caretaker and I was excellent at my job. From the time I was around nine or ten years old, I took care of our big house. I did the cleaning and the laundry, the grocery shopping and cooking, and I took care of my mom.

My mother was not a total invalid, but she was very depressed and physically worn down from all her operations. What she did most of the time was sit and watch television and smoke cigarette after cigarette. Or she would read for hours and smoke cigarette after cigarette. She was a champion worrier! If there was nothing to worry about she'd invent something. When she was younger, before I was born, she was quite athletic. I was told she often went hunting and hiking with my father. She loved to swim and was an excellent diver, and she taught most of us how to dive. In her younger days, she had a zest for life and communication. My mom was even a member of a club called the Jabberwocky Club, because she and my aunts loved to talk so much. But I never saw that side of her. I never saw her well. I hardly ever saw her laugh.

I got to be an expert at denying my feelings. As I was growing up, my pet cats gave me comfort and a feeling of intimacy I missed from my mother and family. Through playing with the cats and taking care of them, I learned a lot about love and affection. They were my friends. I think my connection with them saved me emotionally.

Teenage Years ❧

As I approached my early teens, things went from bad to worse. I saw one of my sisters have a nervous breakdown; she couldn't talk for several days. My father had a nervous breakdown, and my mother went off several times to mental health facilities for weeks at a time. Most of the time I was this little numb body, walking around too scared to feel or talk. I looked up to my older brothers and sisters, yet I felt so isolated from them. I was too young to be included when my brothers and sisters were doing something and our age differences seemed much more pronounced when we were growing up. In our family there is an age span of 15 years from myself to the oldest child.

How I Channeled My Beliefs ❧

Nobody talked about anything or discussed feelings. Everything was always "fine." Through all this confusion I was stuffing my feelings more and more, and the need to gain some semblance of control in my life became more paramount. I became bulimic at age 13 and stayed that way for 14 years. It just happened. I still don't know how, but it did. I do believe it was a way my unconscious mind helped me survive and control my feelings. It was a way for me to process all my unconscious self-hate and anger. On a scale of 1 to 10, if 10 was the worst bulimic you could be, I was probably an 8 or 9. By the time I was 15, I was throwing up four or five times a day. Back then no one knew of or talked about this disorder, so I thought I was absolutely crazy. But I told no one, and I felt powerless to stop. It was a powerful addiction, not unlike drugs. I remember thinking I would have rather been a prostitute than do this disgusting thing each day. Being a prostitute in a good Catholic family, to me, was about the worst thing you could be. That's how bad I felt about being me. I had no control over bulimia and I felt completely worthless.

When I was 14, I started drinking heavily and I would get totally drunk on weekends. I would fast all day, and then at night I would chug three cans of beer, enough to get me thoroughly drunk. I started to smoke cigarettes and marijuana at 15.

I also tried to kill myself twice, once consciously and

once unconsciously. Repressing all my feelings was taking its toll! My two incidences of attempted suicide occurred at 15. At that time my mother was really dependent on me. She had no one else with whom to relate, and she used me to vent all her frustrations. She'd be yelling at me all the time. I had heavy responsibilities, but my parents didn't balance my responsibility with social activities. I had to argue and fight for any normal teen fun. I was really made to feel guilty for wanting to enjoy life and have fun.

For a time, my father must have seen what all this tension was doing to me, because he let me live at a girlfriend's house for about a month while I recuperated from mononucleosis. During my stay, I saw what normal family life was like. The people who let me stay with them were great. They talked to their kids and related to their lives. I got to feel what it was like to be loved openly and completely.

They had seven kids living in this little house with one bathroom. I felt more peace and relating going on there than I ever did at my house. I never wanted to go back home. One night my girlfriend and I got drunk. It was a very cold winter night in upstate New York, all the feelings that had been hidden in my heart started to surface, and most were feelings of hopelessness.

That night I felt so bad about my life that I started banging my head against the wall of their family room. Her parents were gone, and I was definitely out of control. I then tried to run outside and freeze myself, remembering something my mother told me when I was little. She told me people die in the snow because it is easy to fall asleep and freeze to death before they wake up. I thought that sounded like a painless way to go. I knew, being so drunk, I could fall asleep without too much effort. But my friend had enough on the ball to stop me and calm me down.

Depths of Despair ❧

My self-depreciating behavior was not new; I had been thinking about suicide on and off for several years. On previous occasions, I would take butcher knives out and look at them and wonder how it would feel to stab myself or cut my wrists. I was also leaving lots of little doodles on paper about death and killing myself. One day my brother Robert saw some of these, and he brought them to my mother's attention. But she never talked to me about those cries for help, and I continued to think of killing myself.

Another time I almost died was when my boyfriend invited me to his junior prom. I was a sophomore at the time, and going to the junior prom was a big deal. Well, we went to the dance and had dinner, double-dating with another couple. The other boy was in college, and he invited us to his dorm to drink after dinner. Of course I said yes, and off we went. I always chugged my drinks very fast then, so I could get roaring drunk. I drank about a quart of whiskey sours and a bottle of champagne, and in no time I was unconscious for at least six hours. They called in a medic at one point because I had stopped breathing. My date had to carry me out of the dorm. As he was carrying me, I was screaming at the top of my lungs, "Help me, help me." Because I was unconscious, I didn't remember a thing.

When they dropped me off at my house at five in the morning, I still couldn't see straight. My mother never noticed or even commented on my torn and vomit-stained dress. I literally crawled up the stairs to my bed. Nothing was ever said about that incident. My cry for help went unnoticed!

But something had snapped in me shortly after that night, and I knew I wanted to live. I also knew if I stayed at home I wouldn't survive, so I ran away. I had thought about running away from home since I was eight, and I constantly talked about it to my girlfriend. Then one weekend, I packed some clothes in a paper bag and I took the bus to my oldest brother's house in the city.

Being the ever-responsible person I was, I called my parents and told them where I was. While I was talking to them and trying to explain why I had to leave, the phone was on my knee and I was shaking so much from fear and nerves that the phone almost crashed to the floor, but all I felt was numbness. A short time later, my brother gave me two weeks to find another place to live. He never explained why he kicked me out to find a place of my own. I had just turned 16!

My Awakening 🐦

I was totally on my own. My parents didn't give me money or emotional support. My brothers and sisters were wrapped up in their own dysfunctional stuff and weren't available to support me in any way, either. I was alone. It was the loneliest time of my life! I felt abandoned by the whole world, but I still wanted to live and find happiness.

What saved me was the realization I was responsible for my life. I started finding answers to my life and life in general. I had always been a deep-thinking child, even as far back as the second grade.

I realized somehow I had created these awful experiences in my life. Reading books about self-help and self-awareness helped me clarify how and why I had experienced what I had. Doing Spiritual contemplations gave me inner strength to help dig myself out of the cesspool I was in. I really felt life came down to two choices: to kill myself directly or indirectly, which meant living my life as a victim, or being in charge of my life and becoming happy. I chose to take charge.

Understanding Free Will ❧

I learned we are born into circumstances that help us grow; present-life circumstances are results of past actions which are perfect tools to use for self-discovery and growth. When I read these books, the teachings resonated with something in my own being and I just knew what they were saying was true. Knowing this consciously gave me hope and the tools to radically change my life for the better.

You always have free will to live your life the way you want, whether you are aware of this fact or not. Only when you live your daily life from the consciousness of total responsibility do freedom and love fully emerge in your life and heart.

I think the hardest thing for me and my clients to accept is the understanding that we created all the circumstances in our lives, whether we are happy or unhappy about them. When I understood this truth, I mean when I really got that truth, it changed my life forever. I was ecstatic, because I realized if I created all the misery in my life, then I have the power to change it. I finally had hope. I knew I was no longer at the mercy of circumstances. I have the power to control my life!

Most people lose hope and joy because they feel powerless to change anything in their lives. I know when I teach this spiritual principle to my clients, the ones who accept it and LIVE it change the most and the quickest.

Mastering Your Life ❧

When you live life with the realization that you can consciously be the master of your life, you then can take your life where you want it to go. The key to any change on this planet is incorporating truths into daily life and living those beliefs, not just having an intellectual understanding of them. When you take the teachings that follow and use them, they work. If you read this book and store this knowledge without using it, like so much accumulated mental garbage, then you may be keeping yourself a victim.

Just realizing that in each moment we are creating our future with all our present actions brought me through some of the worst times in my life. I came out of those times stronger, happier, and wiser. In the darkest of times I *knew* my actions made a difference in my life. I kept making my actions positive and value-creating. I knew in my heart, even if I couldn't immediately see results I wanted, the results were still being created on some level in my life, and eventually the results would manifest on the physical level.

Some people have to be in the dumper before they allow themselves to see a truth or live a truth. That was the case in my life. If I hadn't had the pain and struggles in my earlier life, I don't think I would have pursued the deeper truths of life and God.

So no matter where you are in your life or what you are experiencing, it is up to you to take responsibility for the outcome of your life experience. It's what you do NOW that counts. This is truly living life responsibly. Find out for yourself how your actions can change your life.

Truth is not someone telling you something is this way or that way. Truth needs to be experienced, and it's up to you to experience it. And for that, you have to be responsible and put these or other teachings that resonate truth for you into actions. Responsibility is a partner with action. If you get nothing else from this book, I hope you understand the actions of your thoughts, emotions, and physical being are actually creating your life. For you to create the life you want, absolutely know you can change anything you want in your life. You have created all that is in your life now. You can now be a conscious director of your life and create it any way you dream is possible!

Beliefs

The time has come
in one man's Soul,
to start his journey
on the road to know . . .

Step by step she goes
forward, forward, ever forward;
seeing now what she didn't before
reality always present . . .

New worlds greet him
with open arms
all rejoicing that he has come,
for the worlds have always been there,
waiting . . .

In her amazement she is confused,
for what she left she thought was the truth.
As she allows the new world to filter
through,
more and more she sees the new view . . .

Nothing has ever been hidden before
he just never traveled this far, was all.
For the new worlds are there for all to see
manifesting only for those who believe! ❦

Chapter 2

Beliefs

There are still many mysteries to this life. I believe we are evolving into to a new age of human consciousness! During this century there has been a reawakening of awareness in the power of thoughts and their effects. In a large part, this change has occurred because we have accepted different ways of viewing our own thoughts. Beliefs about life, and what life is, have changed.

In this chapter, I cover what beliefs are, how they are created, and how you can create more of what you want in your life. The *advanced* beliefs you need to hold to create a more profound way of living are also discussed.

Thoughts and Energy ❧

In this century, more and more people have been exposed to the concept that thoughts and beliefs create reality. These thoughts and beliefs are forms of energy. Beliefs are thought patterns the mind uses to communicate to you and others in this physical universe. Thoughts, no matter how small, are ways in which your mind communicates with you and your environment. (For the rest of this chapter, "thoughts" or "beliefs" mean the same thing.)

Thoughts are like magnets, and they are the building blocks to larger beliefs. An analogy for this is how we use words to express ourselves. Each word means something, and each word is a building block to a larger communication. When you put the words together in an order, as in a sentence, the communication is clearer and deeper than

33

just a single word or phrase. Complex communication, then, is more than single words; it is sentences, paragraphs, or even books.

It is similar with our beliefs. We have many thoughts running through our minds all the time. These individual thoughts are our building blocks to larger, more complex beliefs, which usually are found in your unconscious mind. Your thought patterns bring you what you consistently and completely believe, so the more complex or deeply held your belief is, the harder it usually is to change.

Thoughts are really just different forms of energy. They only seem different than solid things because they have different densities. Besides communication, Soul uses thoughts, through the use of your mind, to help you create on the physical level. Einstein observed that energy is neither created or destroyed, it just changes form. So, everything is created from energy! Your beliefs and thoughts are always transmitting, just as radio waves are always there to be received whether you have your radio on or not. Your thoughts, too, are always transmitting to life, and consequently, they are always creating. Whether you are conscious of your beliefs or oblivious to what you are holding in your mind, your thoughts consistently affect your life. Your life is truly a mirror of what you believe!

What you think and believe determines how you see and interact with life. Your thoughts or beliefs are windows of awareness. If your window is only so big, then you believe that is the only reality. If your window is bigger, you see a bigger picture, or a new aspect to your life. At any point in time, you may feel a particular window is the true aspect of your life, a true representation of reality. Each time you gain in awareness, your belief about what is true about life changes. This is because your window of reality has changed. Reality is really a point of perception of consciousness.

It's like the story of the three blind men. They stood by an elephant and tried to describe it to each other. Each man felt the part of the elephant closest to him. One felt the eyes, one the elephant's tail and the other the elephant's leg. Each felt something true about the elephant. But they had only part of the truth, because their windows of reality (their experiences) were different. What they perceived (or were conscious of at the time) was only part of the truth.

In your life you are like those blind men. You may be blinded to the greater truths of life or limit yourself in what you can achieve by the thoughts you hold. So a great part of changing your reality entails changing *what* you believe. Many people want to change some aspect of their lives, but they don't want to alter their attitudes, thoughts, or actions to accomplish this.

The Mind 🍃

People get caught in the trap of the mind and become lazy when it comes to changing attitudes and beliefs about life. Change requires effort. And to change beliefs about yourself and the world around you necessitates focusing your thoughts consistently on your goal or objective. It means being open to different ways of thinking and attitudes and releasing old patterns that no longer serve you. It means giving yourself the freedom to pick and choose the beliefs that will add the most value to your life. When you live with the flexibility of choosing your beliefs, you can indeed change your life.

Realize the mind is the seat of your thoughts. Your mind is very much like a computer terminal. It is not intelligent by itself; it is the vehicle by which your thoughts are transferred to the physical plane of existence through Soul. Soul is the actual power behind your thoughts. Without Soul, which is your true self, your body wouldn't be able to move or think.

True power comes from Spirit. Humans, especially in this century, seem to worship the intellect as the ultimate power in life. Actually, the intellect is a limited tool used by Soul to function in this dimension. The mind is physical, and its capacity is limited. (Remember, anything physical is intrinsically limited.)

Only Soul or Spirit is limitless. Soul is "above" the mind and the negative patterns that have been created there. Too many of us try to solve problems with intellect alone. No matter how intelligent you are, there comes a time when intellect will fail to conquer your problems. Ultimately, you have to tap into the power of your Soul to completely transcend all the erroneous or limiting patterns of your mind.

Parts of the Mind ❧

Understanding how your mind works is very important in helping change negative beliefs, and it is one of the many tools to help you grow and change. Knowing the basics of how your mind works can help you discover where your beliefs are held and what hold they may have over you.

The mind is composed of the conscious and the unconscious. The conscious part of your mind is the seat of logic and reason. The unconscious mind is the seat of habits and behaviors, and it is the true powerhouse of the two.

When you are born, you are using your unconscious mind almost exclusively. Your conscious mind (logic and reason) doesn't get fully formed until you are about seven years of age. From birth to seven, you absorb beliefs about yourself and your environment very directly into your unconscious mind.

During these early, formative stages, there are no boundaries between you and your environment. The people and things around you seem like parts of you. In your mind, when you are a small child, there is no separation between you and others. At these early stages of development, whatever you experience from others, unconsciously you believe is part of you. I call this developmental mirroring. Your beliefs, then, are formed through the mirroring you receive from your parents, family members, school experiences, television, and all your life experiences. You grow up thinking of these beliefs as truth.

You are very impressionable in those early years. For example, if your parents have low self-esteem, they can pass that belief on to you by how they take care of you, their feelings of themselves, and the examples they set. All parts of you are receptive to the vibrational energy around you. As a child, if the vibrational energy of the people around you is negative or self-abasing, your unconscious mind picks up the belief that *you're* not worthwhile. And those early beliefs form a window of what you feel is real or not real in life.

For example, if you were raised in India, your perception of life would be vastly different than if you were raised in the United States or Japan. Neither is wrong or right, it's just a section of all reality.

Remember, the mind is very much like a computer and computers run from the data that is entered. The computer doesn't question the logic or reason of the data, it just responds until you change the command or the software. The unconscious mind runs on the input it receives without questioning if the material is positive or not. Your unconscious mind has been programmed since birth, and it will continue to run on these programmed beliefs until you change them.

The part of the mind which holds logic and reason is the conscious mind. Through this part you can direct your thinking to help your unconscious mind hold new beliefs.

Once your unconscious mind is programmed, you attract experiences and people into your life in accordance to the beliefs you hold. Thoughts, being energy, vibrate at certain rates of speed, and those vibrations attract like vibrations. This is how you attract to you what you believe. You actually experience that which you hold to be true unconsciously. Truth or beliefs are only relevant to your capacity to be aware. For example, as a child you may have grown up believing in Santa Claus. That was your truth or reality. As you grew in consciousness and knowledge of life, your awareness changed and you were able to incorporate a new set of beliefs about Santa. Your capacity to see new dimensions of life expanded and this growth in awareness helped you change your belief about what is true or real.

Examining Beliefs ❧

On this planet, you react and live from what you believe. You cannot get away from your beliefs. Every thought is a belief; if you have a mind, you will have beliefs! This is how everyone functions in this dimension. The key to your growth and happiness is **what** you choose to believe. You have control over your thoughts, and so you have control over your beliefs—thus your realities. No one pours thoughts into your head or tells you to think this or that. You are in total control of your life, but most of us choose not to exercise this control, or we are unaware we have this control.

Most people believe something when they see it, but in truth it is the exact opposite. **Your reality is a reflection of your beliefs!** If you were raised with the belief money is the root of all evil, then the likelihood of your accumulating wealth is slim, until you change your belief. You may consciously want more money but until you change your unconscious beliefs regarding money, you will not achieve your goal. This is true with every aspect of your life, from your health and relationships to your beliefs of what you think is right or wrong.

So how do you know what beliefs you are holding in your unconscious, the hidden part of your mind? You can know your unconscious beliefs by the circumstances and the situations that are in your life now. For instance, if you want to lose weight and haven't been able to, then somewhere in your unconscious is a belief or set of beliefs that counter your conscious desire. Also, if you want a positive relationship and you keep attracting inappropriate people, then you can be sure you are holding beliefs in your unconscious mind that are keeping you from this goal. Know that whatever circumstances are in your life, they mirror your inner unconscious beliefs about yourself.

Let's look at this case in point. I had a client who came to me to make more money. When Lisa came to me she was making more money and had more friends than ever before, but Lisa wanted to make even more money and have her business grow even larger. During counseling I asked her if she had any conscious beliefs that she would be lonely or people wouldn't like her if she became more successful. What we discovered through hypnotherapy was Lisa *consciously* felt comfortable with success and money.

Her conscious mind, the one with logic and reason, was in perfect accord with what she wanted. Even though she felt there were no unconscious beliefs holding her back, Lisa still couldn't get beyond a certain income. Because hypnotherapy can reach the client's unconscious mind, I suggested to her unconscious mind to release any beliefs through her morning dreams that kept her from making more money. (Dreams, as you will learn, are messages from your deeper unconscious self or from Soul.) The next week, she came in with a dream that symbolized her unconscious beliefs. Lisa saw herself at a fair with lots of people and in the middle of the fair was a tall ladder. She started to climb the ladder. At the top was a box, and she found herself alone at the top. This dream symbolized her deeper feelings about success and money. It said she'd be alone if she were successful. Her unconscious beliefs were in direct conflict with her goal and conscious beliefs. Unconsciously, Lisa was afraid of being alone at the top!

Circumstances in your life are created by the beliefs your mind holds consciously and unconsciously. Your thoughts are intrinsically a part of Cause and Effect. So the more pessimistic your thoughts are, the more negative things you will attract to your life. The more your thoughts are evolved or advanced or (better yet) spiritual in nature, the more your life will reflect those beliefs.

Success and Victim Thinking ❧

Very successful people seem to have common beliefs. Successful people and highly evolved people use their thoughts to create the lives they want. They tend to live with a sense of total responsibility for what happens to them. Even when they don't like what they see, successful people realize they can choose to create what is in their lives and they also choose how they react to circumstances. Those individuals who are the winners and the happiest in life tend to believe they have creative abilities to change their lives. Winners refuse to live as powerless victims!

Victims believe they have no power or control over their circumstances. If you feel you are powerless, you are proclaiming to life, "I am a victim." When you are coming from the powerless victim mode, you attract all the circumstances that reflect being a victim, such as struggle, sickness, poverty, emotional strain, people who treat you badly, etc.

Both ways of thinking are beliefs; no one argues this point. And since we have choices of what to believe in life, why not choose to focus on beliefs that create value instead of suffering?

Always be conscious of your self-talk, your internal dialogue, which ceaselessly marches through your head. Focus your self-talk in the direction that creates value for your life. Because the victim role is easy to get into, victims may not even realize what they are projecting into their lives by their self-talk. For instance, victims usually are worriers. Victims usually believe if they don't worry, something won't turn out right. In actuality, **when you worry you attract what you fear!** (Remember, your thoughts create through Cause and Effect.) By constantly going over something with negative feelings or thoughts, you create a breeding ground for the situation to happen —most probably the very situation you don't want!

When I was a bulimic, I thought constantly about food and my weight. I worried about calories and whether I would gain weight from what I ate. My obsessing intensified the condition I was afraid of and this thought pattern kept weight on me. There is more to healing bulimia then changing thought patterns, but that is a very important part of healing the condition. The thought patterns in my mind when I was a bulimic were stuck. The mind is truly a machine, and I turned my machine into a worry producer and, consequently, a fat producer.

Now, since I've changed those beliefs, I never think about food until I am physically hungry. Those old negative thought patterns were changed by my consistently altering my thinking patterns and basing all my daily actions to live life with a higher awareness. I haven't weighed myself in 11 years, and I am at least one dress size smaller now than I was when I was bulimic. Food is no longer a worry for me and I no longer obsess over it. I can eat anything I want, and I stay at my perfect weight. I actually eat more now than I did when I worried all the time about my weight and obsessed over food.

Worry 🍂

Worry is a thought process filled with tension. Tension causes delay in creating what you want, so worrying can repel what you desire. Let's say you are a whiz at positive thinking and you do it all the time. Positive thinking is done by the conscious part of your mind. If you have inner tension about what you are trying to change in your life, then when you are thinking those positive, conscious thoughts, the deep belief you hold in your **unconscious** mind is that you don't believe you will succeed. *Tension and worry go hand in hand with disbelief.* When you are relaxed about a particular circumstance in your life, you are positive about the situation and you will draw it to yourself quicker. To achieve change, your conscious and unconscious minds have to be in alignment.

The true belief you hold when you worry is that the physical world and all the happenings in it are more powerful than God and Spirit. **You will feel no fear when you are connected to Spirit!** This is a lesson I find myself learning over and over again.

Tension and worry, though, can help you grow. You can use them to help you discover hidden beliefs that keep you from achieving your goals. When you examine what you are worried or tense about, you will discover what your hidden beliefs are.

Being human, it is very easy to fall into this state of consciousness. For me it has been a lifelong battle against the programming I learned from my mother, who worried for a career. My mind and thoughts now are much calmer, I am more positive, and I am definitely more in control of my thoughts. Now when I fall into fear and worry, I get out of that state much more quickly.

Limitations of Mental Reprogramming ❧

My career as a Clinical Hypnotherapist has been devoted to helping other people and myself change unwanted beliefs. When I started this career, I already knew how powerful thoughts and beliefs could be. I had walked barefoot across red hot coals unharmed. I had jumped off a 40-foot telephone pole with a broken hand. (I did have a harness, but I still had to battle my fear of heights). I have also taken many courses that teach ways to help individuals change negative beliefs. I did these things to prove to myself how powerful my mind and beliefs can be.

I went into this profession expecting to see quicker changes and results with my clients than with traditional counseling methods, and I have. But what I didn't expect to find out was the mind can only go so far in helping you to heal and change. I experienced within myself and with my clients a limitation with using only mental tools to heal negative beliefs.

This is the limitation I see with trainings or counseling that focus solely on mental reprogramming. Initiating changes on all levels helps to create advanced changes within the individual. When I started incorporating Spiritual principles into my counseling sessions, greater advancements were achieved. Any good therapist will incorporate principles to help heal an individual's emotions as well as the thought patterns. What most thera-

43

pies or trainings don't do is incorporate Spirit into the healing process.

Spirit is the stuff that makes us...us. When you die, it is because Soul has left the body. Without Soul, your body can no longer function, much less think. Spirit and Soul are more powerful than the mind, thoughts, and beliefs. It just makes sense to use the highest part of yourself to change your other aspects.

This doesn't mean people who only use mental techniques don't get results. On the contrary, many, many people have grown and changed for the better with mental programming and reframing. What I am saying is there may come a time when the mental techniques you have used to change your thoughts and beliefs won't work anymore. This is the time to get above the mind by connecting to your Spiritual self. The true power that affects your mind, emotions, and physical body comes from Soul and God.

Throughout this book, there are techniques to help you change all aspects of yourself: emotional, mental, physical, and spiritual. Reading this book and trying to consciously understand and incorporate its teachings into your life will do much to change your beliefs about reality. As your beliefs about reality change, the actions you make with your thoughts, words, and deeds will change. Your environment will then start to reflect those changes as well.

Mass Consciousness Beliefs 〰

All the people on this planet send out thought waves of energy. When these thoughts are focused on the same thought or perceived reality, this is called a mass consciousness belief. This can be a collective belief of a single group of people or even all the people on this planet. At any given time, it is a group that shares a reality. It is important to know about mass consciousness beliefs so that you can live with freedom of choice. Too many of us lead our lives guided by advertising and societal rules instead of individually choosing what is right for our lives. If you don't know you are reacting from a mass consciousness belief, you cannot be in a position to choose what you want to believe. And you can only grow as Soul when you are free to be your individual self living your life from the point of creator, not someone who is lead.

The energy of this shared reality is sometimes very difficult to not take on and believe. Living the way you feel is best for you and encouraging change within yourself can be difficult. The more you allow yourself to live based on beliefs that serve your highest good, the more you can create a life that is right for you, not the life someone else wants for you. At times you may be the only one who has the consciousness to live a more advanced way. Because we are social creatures, it can be hard to be different or to be the first to live and act from a different belief.

It takes courage and fortitude to grow and open up to new realities. People of this planet once believed the world was flat; that was the mass consciousness belief of that time. When Christopher Columbus left to sail to India, people thought he was crazy to travel further than was previously known. Most people of his day thought he would fall off the end of the Earth. But he was true to his inner urgings and believed the world was round. He helped change the concept of reality of his world. He now has a place in history because he literally broadened the mass consciousness belief of his time.

Everyday, we are faced with mass consciousness beliefs we take as truth. They are so pervasive we may forget or not even realize we don't have to believe them. These beliefs can be handed down from parent to child and, as children, we don't usually question what we are taught. Many people may still think the beliefs they were taught are the only reality. Many of my clients are amazed when I tell them they no longer have to believe certain "truths" from their past. They come to find out that what they had thought was truth was, in reality, a belief they were taught.

One very simple mass consciousness belief I work with all the time is: people always gain weight when they quit smoking. Most of my clients think this is true. Some people do, in fact, gain weight when they quit smoking. But the point is you **do not** have to gain weight. The weight gain is just a belief. When I quit smoking, I decided not to adopt that belief. I actually lost weight when I quit smoking!

Changing Beliefs 🙠

People hold beliefs for various reasons. Most people don't realize their beliefs can be changed. Just because you have always believed something doesn't mean you have to for the rest of your life. Just knowing you can believe anything you want is very liberating.

Adopting new beliefs can also be very frightening. Lots of people don't want to change their thought patterns because they are afraid of change, of the unknown. Many people are comfortable with what is known to them, even if what is known causes them unhappiness.

Most people keep beliefs because they don't know how to change their thought patterns. I teach people who are unaware about the nature of their thoughts and help them become enlightened to new possibilities. I give guidance so they can change negative thought patterns, but I cannot help anyone who refuses to change. If you want to change badly enough, you will be presented with the tools for achieving that change. Whether it is from this book or someplace else, the answers will come to you. Then it is up to you to use them. You are the master of your own destiny. It comes down to what kind of life you want.

Power of Positive Expectation 🙢

Here are some basic ways to use thoughts to achieve your goals and desires. Remember that your realized goals and desires are thoughts and beliefs you've held with consistency and feeling. One basic belief successful people use to create their goals is the power of positive expectation. Positive expectation is looking forward to the prospect of success in the future. It is anticipating realized results. Some people expect the positive, while others expect and focus on the negative. You always attract that which you expect! Most people just don't realize they are *always* in the state of expectation.

When you want to create a new situation for yourself, the likelihood of success is increased by the amount of energy you put into positive expectation. Successful people consciously focus on what they want out of life—they fill themselves with positive expectation. Arnold Schwarzeneggar is a wonderful example of someone who consciously uses positive expectation. He has said he knew his name would be world known. He *expected* it to happen; by keeping his mind focused on his expectation, he realized his desire. Another shinning example of positive expectation is Carol Burnett. Someone asked her one time if she expected to be successful as an actress when she first started out. She replied she *always* expected to be successful. So when embarking on new adventures, try to keep your outlook filled with positive expectancy.

EXERCISE

Learning How to Visualize

One vehicle of positive expectation is using the power of visualization consciously. Whether you are aware of it or not, we all visualize every day. When we daydream about a loved one or where we want to go for dinner, we are actually visualizing. The process can be as simple as filling yourself up with a feeling of what you want to experience, for example, like the feelings of positive expectation you feel when you're going to meet a loved one. Many people can only imagine seeing themselves in the meeting. But that is only one part of the visualizing process.

The more real you imagine something to be, the closer you will come to achieving it. The more senses you use, the better. In the example of meeting a loved one, visualize where you want to go for dinner, using all your senses to make your imagery more real. This could include hearing conversation and feeling the texture of the tablecloth. Imagine smelling the aromas of the food you are about to eat, and all the feelings you have about the person you are with. Create details with your visualization of the room and all the things around you. You can do this same procedure with anything you want in life.

The next step would be to put the visualization in the present moment. Assume you have it now, whatever your particular "it" is. Put the desire in your mind for the good of all and yourself. Then release the manifestation of your desired objective to Spirit.

Let me give you another example. Suppose you have always been in a salaried job, and you start to seriously think about starting your own business.

First, assume you can have your desire. Get very clear on what you want to do. Know the major aspects of what you want. For instance, see the kind of people you'd like to work with, the income you'd like to make, if you want to travel, etc.

Next, imagine yourself in the business and use as many senses as possible to make it real to you. Put it in the present moment because your thoughts create only in the now. If you constantly feel like your desires are in the future or you say to yourself, "I will get there someday," you are programming your mind to get your desire in the future. And the future really never comes. There is only the eternal now. Then put all your feelings and visualizations in the present moment.

Ask Spirit to send you the perfect business for your growth and happiness and for the good of all. The phrase "for the good of all" is very important, because with it you are releasing control over other people or Spirit. When you phrase your desires this way, you are insuring development from your highest self, and the likelihood of incurring negative karma is lessened.

When you release control of the outcome to Spirit, you become a partner with Spirit. When you are open to Spirit, Spirit is always in your life to manifest whatever is necessary for your highest good. The more you trust this truth, the happier you will be. Your ego does not always know or care what is for your highest good or the good of others. When you ask for something using this phrase, you are coming from your higher self. Please remember, Spirit will always manifest for your highest good and for the good of the whole of life.

Be assured all things are being brought to you in the quickest fashion. By releasing your desires to Spirit, you are reaffirming the highest power is Spirit, not your mind or anything physical. Always know Spirit will do only what is best for your growth. **In *no* way will Spirit lessen your life.** ❧

Working With Spirit

A great visualization to do to work with Spirit is one where you put all your thoughts and feelings about what you want into a pink cloud. Let's say you want a new career or business. See yourself happy in every aspect of a new career. Picture yourself making the amount of money you want and being around the kind of people you like. Use all of your senses. Next, see that cloud rising into the sky with all your feelings, thoughts, and visualizations about what you want to create. Then see it disappear. The pink color represents love, and the cloud represents the effortless way in which you release your goals to Spirit. ❧

Next, take actions to bring your business or whatever you want into a reality, trusting in the power of Spirit. Try to put yourself in a place where you no longer need or feel anxious about your goal. The more you let go of the feeling of need, the faster things will manifest for you.

Before I started my hypnotherapy career, I had a very clear idea I wanted to work with people and, at the same time, have a business with which I could grow and change. I wanted to be able to make a certain amount of income and I wanted to *always* love and enjoy my work. I did not ask Spirit to give me such-and-such business or to take anything away from anyone else. I just knew the perfect career would manifest itself even when there were no visible signs apparent to me. I held on to the **expectation** that my perfect business would manifest, and it did. These techniques really work!

Receiving ❧

Another important point that can keep you from changing and getting what you want is being blocked about *receiving*. Anything you want is, in reality, just energy. To grow and change, you must be open to this energy to enter into your life. Thoughts are energy, and you must be aware of letting your old beliefs go to be able to RECEIVE abundance in the form of new, positive, enabling beliefs. The more you are open and receptive to the beliefs which are in harmony with what you want, the faster you manifest your desires.

Many people complain they are not accomplishing their goals. One basic reason for this is they shut off their abundance. Most are unaware they don't know how to receive. To grow fully, we must have a balance between giving and receiving. This balance is really a flow of energy.

If you are constantly making goals about money and you don't acknowledge and accept other forms of abundance, like unexpected help, a gift, or a compliment, you might have a problem with receiving. Spirit, which is total abundance, will only flow to where there is acceptance or openness.

The primary reason for lack of acceptance is the basic belief we are not worthy. When we feel lovable and worthy, we can accept all the good things life has to offer.

Throughout this book, you will find ways to help you live your life from a deeper and more positive place. Know beliefs are tools, and you can use these tools in any way you want. You have choices, and you have the power to change. This is the most empowering belief you can consistently hold. **You, as Soul, are limitless!**

Our True Purpose

Who am I?
Where am I going??
What am I doing???
Not Now!
NOT Me!!
God.....NOT THIS!!!!
Why me? Why ME? WHY ME???
AARRRRGGGHHHHH!!!!!!!!!!!!!!!!!
I can't STAND IT any more!!!

Nothing in my life makes any
sense............I guess............
Well......I guess I could.
If only I would,
If I CHOOSE to
grow myself,
to the highest place.
within myself.
THEN I could.........
see what it means,
to REALLY be,
ME! ≈

Chapter 3

Our True
Purpose of Living

Who are we and what are we living for? These
are not easy questions to answer. Ultimately, you have to
answer these questions for yourself from your own inner
searching and experience of truth. Truth is to be experienced. It is not just knowledge stored away someplace in
your mind.

You As Soul ❧

Simply stated, you are Soul. You are not a body with
a soul, you ARE Soul. Soul is a happy, joyful, loving entity.
For now, realize that you are Soul and, as Soul, you are an
individualized and unique expression of God. We are all
part of God.

Most people were raised with the concept that we are
a body that has a soul. In truth, it is the exact opposite.
We have a body to give Soul a vehicle to live in this plane
of existence, the physical level of being, the planet Earth.

When you start to live from the perspective that your
true self is Soul, then a shift in your awareness occurs.
You look at life a little differently and you start to make
life choices based on this awareness. The real meaning
and purpose of your life starts to peep through your mind
and your daily routine takes on new meaning. The reason
most of us don't live from this higher understanding is
because we get caught up in the day-to-day routine of living. Just concentrating on the mundane physical aspects
of life tends to block out knowledge and consistent aware-

ness of God and the Spiritual nature and purpose of life. Absorption in daily life can separate you from the knowledge that your true self is Soul. When you start to live your life from this elevated awareness, you realize you are more than your body, thoughts, or achievements. You are Soul!

Why Is Soul Here? ❧

Why then is your Soul in a body, and why are you having this life? What does it mean to have an elevated awareness, and what does "that" have to do with your happiness? So what does all of this mean?

Soul uses the body as a vehicle to experience the physical level of existence. I use the phrase, "physical level of existence," because there are many different realities or planes of experience besides the planet Earth. In essence, your Soul is on Earth to learn to become a co-worker with God. Now that may sound like complete drudgery or bring up feelings of oppression to some of you, but the more you unify your purpose with God and Spirit, the more love you experience and the happier you become. This is because God and the essence flowing from Him (Spirit) is pure LOVE! When you are unified with love, how can you not be happy, no matter what else is going on around you?

The state of awareness that is a co-worker with God is like being a single drop of water in the ocean. You may be only one drop, but when you unify with the ocean, you have the strength and power of the total ocean. The same holds true with individual consciousness. When we unify our purpose with that of Spirit and God, we can eventually have ITS power coursing through us. Separating our purpose or consciousness from that "biggest" reality, so to speak, limits what we can experience and achieve.

Or you can view being a co-worker like the Native Americans who saw themselves as intrinsically linked with Mother Earth. They lived in harmony with the laws of nature, and there was peace and harmony to their existence. Being a co-worker with God is simply following the highest and happiest way of living. It is going with the flow of life instead of swimming against it.

Your individual Soul needs many experiences to develop as a co-worker with God. This is a state where Soul functions from total love for itself and all of God's creatures. This takes effort on Soul's part and many lifetimes of learning to achieve. When you live as God's co-worker, you realize there is no separation between you, God, and all of life. What you do for others and yourself does affect the totality of life.

Reincarnation Revisited! 🍂

It's hard to further discuss Soul's need for different experiences without explaining reincarnation in more depth. Reincarnation, on the Earth plane, is Soul experiencing different lifetimes by being born again and again into different physical bodies. Through reincarnation, your Soul gains experiences it needs in order to achieve a greater understanding of God and to develop its capacity for love, wisdom, charity, and service.

Through each incarnation, or new lifetime, you (Soul) accumulate a deeper understanding of spiritual principles and develop your capacity to love and to be a **fully conscious** part of Spirit. Even though you've had many different lives, both as men and women, your Soul keeps its identity intact. When you are reborn, a filter comes over your mind so your past lives are not easily apparent. (Otherwise, your present mind would get confused, and not accomplish much of anything in this life.)

Starting each lifetime fresh and unaware of previous lifetimes is like starting your day with a fresh attitude.

When you start each day as a new beginning, unencumbered by the previous day's happenings, you can make stronger and more positive actions each day. Similarly, as Soul, you start a new life with fresh challenges to spur you on the road to knowing and experiencing God. Hopefully you are accumulating more good karma than bad, and through your experiences, a greater understanding of Spirit with each life. This understanding comes through and helps you develop a more positive life when you live each moment with truth and Spirit to the best of your abilities.

Your Evolution ❧

The example of your growth and development as a human is similar to your Soul's own development. You start out as a baby learning how to walk and talk. Then you go to school to learn lots of different subjects necessary for your adulthood. During this time you interact with new people and learn new social skills. Each stage of life teaches you something necessary to help you grow and develop. One level of learning makes way for a more advanced level, and so on.

Without your experiences as a baby and a toddler, it would be nearly impossible for you to develop new skills necessary for your advancement as an adult.

Soul's reincarnation is a similar process. You as Soul were born from God, and God has placed you on your journey of growth experiences to gain wisdom. God wants you to be happy and for you to be all you can be. Just as a baby is born self-absorbed and innocent of the workings of life, so too is Soul. As individuals need many different kinds of situations to develop into capable and compassionate adults, Soul needs these varied experiences of different lifetimes to develop wisdom, love, and compassion for all of life.

"As Above So Below" ❧

There is an old saying: "As above, so goes below." Change and growth start with higher spiritual knowledge, which filters down to the human state of consciousness. Changes which occur in your Soul affect all aspects of your life now. Also, your individual life now mirrors the development from your Soul's previous reincarnations.

So why does Soul travel this route to know God? In the human state of consciousness, there will always be questions that we can't answer. Our world is material, and its nature is intrinsically limited. Never will you or anyone else know God or the workings of life completely from the intellect. You have to go above your emotions and mind, straight to your true self as Soul, in order for you to realize and fully be connected to God and what life is all about. This is God-Realization.

God-Realization ❧

The state of God-Realization is an elevated state of awareness. This state is a direct knowing and communion with God, the Holy Spirit, or the Totality of Life—whatever you feel comfortable calling IT. This communion is not achieved with your intellect, but through a direct link with Soul and Spirit. It's achieving and *being* in this state in the human form before you leave your body at death. It's experiencing a little bit of heaven on Earth!

Experiencing heaven on Earth does not mean that you will never experience problems, difficulties or emotions. God-Realized people look pretty much the same as anyone else, and they tend to all the normal day-to-day stuff that the rest of us do. God-Realized individuals can be laborers or world leaders. What has changed for them is their inner selves and their inner awareness and connection to Spirit. Their intention, direction and purpose for life has evolved and changed. They are consciously leading lives in harmony with the higher purpose of Spirit and God. And they are doing this with their everyday lives. Their inner joy, happiness, and experience of love is not dependent on what is happening in their outer lives, because they have a direct link with Spirit, love, and the truths of life.

To serve God and achieve the higher states of awareness, it is **not** necessary to separate yourself from friends, family, or the things you love to do. **What is necessary is the intention you hold in your heart while you are living your life.** The more you evolve and the more you consciously live your life in the name of God, the more your life becomes truly meaningful. Anything less is just mechanical action to cover the wants of your ego and your body. Your ego and your body do end, but Soul is immortal. The more you do just for the sake of your body or your ego, no true lasting happiness can result! This is true because your focus is on something that has no permanence; your body and ego will one day die, but you as Soul are immortal. This doesn't mean for you to never do things for your physical self or to become a martyr; I mean shifting your focus while you are living daily life.

Inner and Outer Self ❧

The key to achieving a truly purposeful, happy life is to consciously dedicate your daily life to this higher purpose—connecting to Spirit in your daily workings of life. Highly-evolved Souls live each moment awakened to Spirit, their inner growth, and their mission or purpose on Earth. Your awakening affects your daily life by the actions that you take and from the deep intentions you keep in your heart. This awareness may be with your outer consciousness, in your inner self, or both.

The inner part of a person is unseen, like emotions. The outer part of a person is the physical body and what can be seen with the physical eyes and felt with the other senses. The outer part of life is what most of us center on. It's what most people think is the only reality. **True happiness and growth are achieved from your inner self, your inner awakening.** When you focus on your inner awakening, then the inner change that manifests will effect change in your outer life. Change in your outer environment is always preceded by some kind of change within your inner self which is made up of your emotional, mental, and spiritual parts of yourself.

Soul's Mission ⫯

Just as each Soul is different and unique, so too is its mission or purpose. Each Soul has a mission for Spirit and God. When you live your life from your heart dedicated to God or the Divine of life, all missions are important. Neither is better nor greater than the other. You are then willingly led by Spirit, and IT uses you where your talents are needed. You are **not** giving up your free will or individuality when this happens. You realize this is the happiest way to live and you **willingly** partake in Spirit's direction. It is similar to floating down a river with the current instead of fighting against it. Spirit is always leading you to your highest happiness and good. Flow with It. When you truly understand this, you will happily be led by this Divine direction.

To live a fully awakened life, compared to an average life, is like comparing a baby's awareness of itself and life to that of a fully-grown adult. The person is the same, but the consciousness is at different stages of development.

The baby is consciously unaware of its surroundings and what life means; the baby reacts and depends on its parents for survival. Babies are limited in their freedom to move, and so they are limited in what they can experience. They view reality in a very different way than fully-grown adults. Both are in the same body and the same world. What has changed is their growth and awareness. Physical, mental, and emotional growth has to take place for the baby to become a fully-functioning adult.

To grow as Soul, the same kind of growth has to take place within your consciousness and deep within yourself. We all have free will to live our lives the way we want. You can choose to allow yourself to mature and grow within your spiritual self, or you can choose not to grow.

So, if you do choose to grow in spiritual awareness, how do you accomplish this? How do you connect with yourself as Soul to get what you need in order to grow toward a higher self-realized state of awareness or God-Realization?

Changing your awareness of life entails knowing where you are now. I tell my clients being aware of obstacles is the first step in growing. It's similar to diagnosing an illness. Without knowing what your illness is, how can you treat it?

Growing As Soul ❧

Your first step, then, in growing as Soul is to acknowledge you are Soul. The next step is to develop your awareness of truth and Spirit and then connect to God or the Divine in this lifetime. The more you come from your inner direction to know God and Spirit, the more God and Spirit flows through your being and life.

This desire is not a whim, where you try on a spiritual principle for a few days or a few months. The desire I am talking about is an ongoing quest. It is changing your perception of what is important in your life. It is truly understanding that what is real and important is Spirit and Divine love. The actions you take in your life from that point on will be geared to knowing greater truths, and your intention will be on incorporating those truths with all of your being.

No one can grow for you. To grow in Spirit means taking complete responsibility for your life. You have in some way, shape, or form created all the happenings in your life. Now it is up to you to create the actions necessary to achieve spiritual growth. Without living responsibly in the very deepest sense of the word, you cannot expect to see your life evolve past material consciousness.

Many people have come to me for counseling and therapy. The people who grow the most take hold of what I teach and apply it to their daily lives. They are action-oriented people. They work to overcome their problems and achieve their goals. The people that receive very little or no results from therapy are those who want me to "fix" them. They will not incorporate their new-found knowledge into their daily lives. They think hearing the answers to their problems will make their troubles go away. Remember, no one can fix you or grow for you. You have to fix yourself and be in charge of your own growth.

Many people who search for God and happiness put very little effort into their spiritual selves. A great many people put more effort into entertainment and superficialities than their spiritual development. They hope God or someone will come along and magically change their lives for them. Or they think that if other people would change, then they would be happy. Or if a particular circumstance was different, then their lives would have meaning.

Lasting happiness is found by getting a greater and

greater connection with your true self as Soul and living out your true purpose. The way to happiness and growth is to develop your spiritual self. This is not done by wishing or hoping but by taking consistent actions. When you do this, your outer world starts to smooth out and become more harmonious and joyful. Difficult circumstances take on a new meaning and purpose when you are coming from that deeper sense and awareness. The hard things in life get easier to handle when you live from this perspective.

Religion and Spiritual Practice ❧

The way I have found to connect to my Spiritual self is through spiritual practice. Many people are taught that if they go to church once or twice a week and listen to someone preach, they are taking care of their Soul and spiritual unfoldment. They may be. But to reach the state of God-Realization, you need a consistent spiritual practice that will charge and vitalize your life daily. So be honest with yourself about what you are receiving from your present religion or practice. This is vital!

Your religion or spiritual practice should be part of your *daily* life, not just an afterthought you stuff into a little niche in your week. Change and growth occur in the now, the moment. So how you live and believe is of the utmost importance. Your religion should help you become more of an individual and help you connect with Spirit now in your daily life. If your practice, religion, or belief is doing this for you now, great, stay with it. Give yourself the permission to practice the religion or belief that honors yourself, Spirit, and Soul. Don't follow a belief out of guilt or habit.

There are many paths to God. Wherever you are is perfect for your present awareness or you wouldn't be there. You are always having the experiences in your life you need for your development, and this includes the religion or spiritual practice you are using now. Ultimately for your own growth, you have to be willing to let go of any teaching that is no longer serving you or helping you to grow in your daily life. Remember, growth is living life as consciously as possible, on all levels: emotionally, mentally, physically, and spiritually. It is a commingling of Spirit in your daily life. This commingling should have a powerful, positive, and practical impact on your daily life.

My Spiritual Evolution 🍂

My own spiritual evolution started out with Catholicism, which was perfect for my life when I came into this world. My parents were very devout Catholics. And if you know anything about that religion, you know there is an emphasis to stay in it or you'll be damned to "hell." It's intimidating, to say the least.

As my search continued, the Catholic Church's doctrine could no longer answer all my questions about life; neither did it help me feel connected to God. At 15, I left the Catholic church. This was a major decision. I had to follow my heart and do what I felt I needed for my own life. I didn't want to practice a religion just because my parents believed it to be the truth. I had to experience truth for myself.

Then came the brief period in my life when I considered myself to be an atheist. I totally rejected God, Spirit, and all religion. I was on my own at the time, and it was a very dark period in my life. I kept observing life, though, and things I experienced and observed showed me there had to be some kind of larger intelligence in charge. I couldn't deny it. I felt there had to be a Source of all creation.

Then came my agnostic period. Agnostics believe there is a possibility of a God or higher intelligence, but they don't accept formalized religion. This period, which lasted two or three years, helped me have a little more peace, but I still felt a lack of connection to a Source, to Spirit. During this time I read a lot of self-help books, and I came across some very eye-opening spiritual teachings that talked about how in every moment each person creates the future by actions in the present. I had begun to believe in this spiritual principle myself, even before I read the books. The books just confirmed to me the truths I was already starting to know from my own observations.

During this time I tried learning how to meditate. The books suggested I sit still and make my mind blank, something I could never do. Either I got so still that I fell asleep, or I never reached the place of stillness that was supposed to help you connect with God. So meditation was something I did infrequently, at best. But I knew I needed to have a way to connect with Spirit consistently, so I could raise my thoughts and energy above the negative hubbub, vibrations, and energy of the outer world.

About that time, along came Greg. We started to date when I was about 25, and a year and a half later we got married. Our marriage was based in friendship and spiritual growth and we are still good friends today. We divorced when we both realized we had grown as much as we could from our marriage, and we grew a lot from our knowing each other. We were both teacher and student, and he was the one who introduced me to an active spiritual practice, a sect of Buddhism. This sect of Buddhism taught about the effects and power of your thoughts and actions in your daily life, that with each action you create your future. I found these teachings were in agreement with everything I'd come to know from my own observations.

I found Buddhism to be a spiritual practice I could stay awake with! It involved singing or chanting a high vibratory word. You chant this word every day for a period of time that feels comfortable for you. The act of using your voice in this manner helps to raise your vibrations, to change your energy toward the positive, toward your higher self.

So began my Buddhist period. It helped me tremendously. Through this next evolutionary step in my consciousness, I was able to stop being bulimic without therapy! This was a tremendous and powerful experience for me. Understand, I had been a bulimic for 14 years. Nothing I had done stopped my urge to binge and purge, but raising my spiritual awareness and energy did!

That taught me the value of a viable spiritual practice and the power of connecting daily to your higher self. A spiritual practice, to me, is a particular tool to reach your higher self and Spirit every day. It is not an isolated cry for help when things are rough; it is a tool you use with consistency and commitment for your advancement of consciousness and union with Spirit. It is similar to good musicians or athletes who practice every day to become more skilled in their art. If a spiritual practice is working for you, it will positively affect your daily life and help you to have the courage to confront personal issues you may need to change in order to grow. There should be no separation from your spiritual awareness and your daily life. What I found was when I was not consistent with my spiritual practice, I functioned only partially. For me, it was like a car running on only two cylinders, or thinking you can have a perfect body without consistent good food and exercise. Buddhism taught me that in order to reach my goals, spiritual or otherwise, I had to be consistent with my actions. It is necessary to be consistent from beginning to end with thoughts, emotions, and physical movements to achieve your desired results. You are either going forward or backward. There is no standing still!

Spiritual Practice and Prayer ❧

There is a difference between a spiritual practice and typical prayer. Prayer can be a spiritual practice or it can be a way to stay a victim. Most people pray by begging God or Spirit to help them out of some kind of unpleasant circumstance. When people pray as beggars, their energy actually separates them from the Source of life. When people pray in this fashion, it is not a spiritual practice.

A spiritual practice is a tool to use every day, not just when you are feeling down. When you are using a spiritual practice, your goal is to become more connected to God and Spirit, so you can live your life from the energy of cause, which is a creative, active place. When you beg, even to God, you are a victim.

Any form of spiritual practice or prayer should empower your life if your inner intention is one of being the master of your life, in union with Spirit. When you are consciously taking actions to produce what you want in your life, you are living as the initiator, not the victim. Often people pray for years without realizing they are still taking actions that keep them powerless victims.

Changing My Spiritual Practice ❧

Practicing Buddhism helped me feel and act out of the positive and helped me live life with the awareness that my actions were making a difference. This was a very empowering place to be.

I was consistent with my spiritual practice every day, until I reached the inner knowing that it had taken me as far as it could. I felt I had learned all I could from it, and I was wanting and needing a different spiritual practice. So as quickly as I accepted Buddhism, I left. That was a hard decision to make because of the social pressures from my years

68

of practice with the other Buddhists who were my friends. But I knew in my heart I had to search for more answers.

For several years I searched for my next step in growth. I definitely wanted a spiritually active discipline. I learned from Buddhism that it is important for me to have a spiritual practice; otherwise, it can become very easy to get caught up in the mundane workings of daily life. By this time I knew if I kept asking from my heart for the right vehicle to appear for me, that it would. Well, it did, and it's called Eckankar, and I continue to practice it today.

Teachings As Soul ✒

Eckankar teaches you how to contact the Holy Spirit or the Source of all life, directly. Through the spiritual exercises in Eckankar, your consciousness is developed so you can awaken to *experience* yourself as Soul. The result is an increase in freedom, wisdom, and love in your life. Using the high vibratory words it teaches helps you to open your heart and life to love, which in the truest essence is God.

As my awareness expanded, I needed to let go of spiritual vehicles that no longer served me. If I feel the same way in the future about Eckankar, if I should feel that it is not fulfilling my needs in my spiritual or outer life, I will then let it go. So far, I've never grown as fast or with as much joy and love as I have with this spiritual discipline.

None of my experiences with any of spiritual paths was wrong. At the time, they were perfect for my growth and the lessons I needed.

It takes courage to leave the known for the unknown. It is easier to be complacent and stay in familiar thought patterns and experiences than to branch out and try something new. How many times have you tried something new and were frightened of that experience beforehand, but once you tried it you liked it and soon you became comfortable with it? A new way of thinking is no different.

Spiritual Unfoldment ❧

As you grow in your spiritual life, things don't necessarily get easier. Sometimes things seem worse than they were before you started on you road to spiritual growth. Relax if you can, and know you ARE growing in the right direction whenever you focus on your spiritual unfoldment or on God.

As you bring more Spirit into your life IT cleanses your negative karma. Your vibrations are going from negative to positive. You are becoming a clear channel for Spirit. The more you take positive actions, the more you will create the positive in your life, even if at the moment you cannot see evidence of that fact.

During this cleansing process, remember in all your past lifetimes you have incurred positive and negative karma. And as you open and grow in Spirit, your negative karma comes up for "restitution." It might be things you did yesterday, last month, or in another lifetime. But if you keep living from the conviction that the actions you take in the now do make a difference, eventually you will see the results of your positive efforts. Your awareness of life and how you live your life from this expanded consciousness is so much more rewarding. It is similar to your life as a baby—it was nice, but limiting. As an adult, you can appreciate life more and you have more freedom than you did as a baby. So it is with spiritual development.

Clarifying the Confusion ❧

Spiritual unfoldment can get confusing, because negative occurrences can happen in your life for various reasons. Perhaps you're focusing on the things you don't want. This causes energy or the vibration for them to come into your life through your physical actions or your thoughts. Or it may seem that negative consequences happen because of positive spiritual actions. These positive actions are accelerating your growth and cause the surfacing or burning off of old negative karma. Or you may have hardships because Spirit is sending you a particular lesson. Maybe on the Soul level, unknown to your conscious self, you have asked to grow or learn a particular lesson. So to grow and learn that lesson, Spirit has sent you a particular experience to evolve.

Sometimes it's hard not to get stuck in asking, "Why is this happening to me?" The best advice I can give you when you feel over-burdened is to get above the chattering of your mind by connecting to yourself as Soul. I do this through the chanting of different high vibratory words and spiritual visualizations. You may need to meditate, chant, or pray, but do something to rise above the energy of your emotions and mind. Remember, when things seem complicated and confusing, you are usually stuck in the workings of the conscious or unconscious mind.

Soul is simple. Soul is happy and peaceful; it is filled with joy. When things are balanced and peaceful and you are relaxed about what is happening, even if you would prefer it happening in a different way, then you are living more from the level of your Soul.

Balancing Your Growth ❧

In harder times, keep taking positive actions. Read something inspirational or do a Spiritual exercise. You might even need to slow down on your Spiritual exercises. I know I tend to want unfoldment now or, better yet, yesterday. Sometimes I get carried away and submerge myself with too many Spiritual exercises. Then negative karma surfaces, and sometimes it can be too much to handle. So I slow down for a day or two. Doing something very different and human, like going to a movie or exercising or just hanging out and being frivolous, sometimes helps balance out my growth and makes my life a little easier.

When your negative stuff surfaces, know you have the answers and solutions within you as Soul. Let yourself listen for the answers and be open to receive them. God and Spirit always are talking to you through other people, things you read, dreams you have, or the synchronistic occurrences you may have easily overlooked. If you are not in touch with your higher self, you may not hear the answers when Spirit is talking. Jesus Christ said, "Ask and you shall receive." So your next step in getting any answer is to ask for it. It is always there to be had, if you take responsibility to hear it, find it, and accept it.

You Are In Charge ❧

You are in charge of your growth and its speed. Spirit gives you only what you can handle, and unfoldment of your true self can be fast or slow depending the actions you take with your heart, mind, and Soul. Changes don't necessarily occur because you are busy making all the "right" actions. Changes occur because you have voluntarily taken Spiritual truth into your consciousness.

To grow spiritually, you need complete freedom. In your outer world, you can be someone who is living the straight and narrow, but from the inner part of you, where it really counts, your spiritual growth may stop if you are making actions just because someone said you should.

Let me give you an example. As a Catholic, I was told that to go to heaven or to become a more loving person, I had to go to mass every Sunday. For a while I did this faithfully and kept all the rules, but I felt I was getting nothing from these activities. If I had continued, I would have accomplished very little, because I wouldn't have been getting what I felt I needed for my own growth.

I want to emphasize this was my particular experience. If you are going to a church and following its precepts and feel filled with Spirit and it helps your life, keep with it. Each of us has to look within to find out what he or she needs to grow at any particular time.

Victim and Victor 🙚

Because I followed my free will in leaving the Catholic Church, I found out for myself what I needed in my life: how I needed to act, and what I needed to experience to unfold spiritually. We all are given that same free will. It is up to you to implement it. Until you use it, you will never be all you could be. You will remain a victim. Your happiness will always depend on what is happening in your environment, because you are not living from your power within. If something is taken away from you, then so goes your joy and peace of mind. That, to me, is not living freely.

Life is change. It is how you react to change that makes the difference in your life and whether you are truly free or bound by the outer picture of your life. Freedom and happiness come from within. Each moment, by your actions, you choose to be a victim or victor. What do you want from your life? The choice is yours. Remember, you are making that choice in each moment, right now!

God

How do you describe
something that IS,
That is ALL,
seen and unseen,
felt and thought?

How do you describe
the unimaginable
and the imagined,
from the heart and mind
and Soul?

How do you describe
limitless light
and the purest of love,
emanating outward to all existence,
past, present, and future?

........the only description then
....................can be,
GOD !!!!

Chapter 4

In Search of God

Understanding God from the intellectual, emotional, and physical parts of ourselves helps to prepare us to know God as Soul now and when we shed our body, mind, and emotions at death. So who or what is God? How will you know when you connect to any aspect of Him? (I use the pronoun "He," but really God is neither masculine nor feminine. God just IS.) These are tough questions that I hope to clarify so you can have some intellectual and emotional awareness of what you may encounter when you grow as Soul. As you delve deeper into these understandings, you will find some aspects of God are based in physical reality and some are from other levels and dimensions.

Knowing God and Spirit is an ongoing evolution, a never-ending process. Even after death, you continue to grow in your awareness of God and all that He is. Let this chapter guide your further exploration of God and His many aspects. Your understanding and realizations of God have to come from within yourself. I share with you my present awareness—it is neither greater nor lesser than the awareness that lies within you. I hope sharing what I have come to know will speed your growth and understanding of God and Spirit and help you concretely in your daily life. I also hope it helps make knowing God a very real experience for you, not something you grasp only on an intellectual level. Remember, your ability to understand life comes from more than just your intellect.

The point of this book is help you learn to center your actions for your highest development and to develop a state of indestructible happiness and awareness. How can you achieve these without understanding and incorporating God into your daily life? God and Spirit are life. You and I are the individual, physical manifestations of Them. When you learn to connect directly to Spirit, your life will open up into new vistas. As we work toward this direct connection, we have to unfold, step by step, on all levels in our awareness of God. Connecting with God emotionally, mentally, and physically is paramount to your lasting and real happiness. This is our preliminary understanding of Him before we know Him directly as Soul.

Over the years, I have seen my clients change faster when they incorporate Spiritual truths in therapy. This is because they work with their whole selves—their minds, bodies, emotions, and spiritual selves.

Coming to know God and the workings of Spirit is a very personal journey. Someone can point the way for you, but only you can travel the road yourself. What you find on that road reflects your consciousness at any particular time in your life. Hopefully we can arrive at a state of consciousness where we have a conscious knowing of God and Spirit from all parts of our being.

God is perfect in all ways. He is always there for us; we just have to be able to comprehend and take in His essence. If you limit your capacity for understanding, then your experience of Him will be limited. When your ability to comprehend Him grows, so will your experience of Him, and Spirit, become greater and more comprehensive.

This situation is similar to having a fine violin. This violin may be the most beautiful-sounding violin in the world. But if your ability to play is on the beginner's level, then the music you can produce is going to be vastly different than that of a master violinist. The violin, in itself, is perfect and has always been that way. What creates the different, beautiful sounds is the ability of the individual playing this violin. Also, hearing different people play the violin gives you new understandings of what is reachable through this instrument. If you heard only people with mediocre talent play this beautiful instrument, you might believe that was the only way it could sound. The same is true regarding my, or other people's, understandings of God and Spirit; it may broaden your capacity to understand and to be aware of new ways to approach your Spiritual journey when you are exposed to different ways of understanding God.

You have to make the effort to reach God and be open to Him, just as the master violinist makes the effort to learn and practice. It takes more than just asking Spirit to come into your life for you to have this awareness. It takes action on all levels of your being. This principle is the same with anything in your daily life you want to accomplish. You start out with desire, and follow through with consistent actions. It is this consistency of actions with your body, mind, and emotions, from beginning to end, that achieves results.

Let me give you an example of what I mean. Let's say you want to lose weight. First you have desire, but just wishing to lose weight is not enough to accomplish your goal. You have to follow up that desire with consistent, appropriate actions, such as eating less, exercising, and handling the emotional problems that may have been a factor in gaining weight.

The same thing is true with your spiritual development. It takes more then just asking for it or desiring it. It takes consistent action.

Aspects of God ❧

Through my many encounters with different spiritual understandings and through my own inner knowing, I feel it is important to understand the different aspects of God. Recognizing and understanding them helps you to know where you are headed, and they can guide you on your journey. They are like a road map to your destination that makes your travel easier and faster.

First and foremost, God is love. This is what He is. Emanating from Him is Spirit, or what some religions call the Holy Spirit. Spirit is the energy that flows from God to the rest of creation, giving it life and form. Spirit is the heart of God. Spirit is the food for all of existence, seen and unseen, physical and spiritual.

Spirit is an extension of God that manifests as sound, light, and love. Sound, light, and love are the forming "stuff" of all the universes. They are the forming and purifying power of life. When you are purified by the sound and light of God, you are more open for love, freedom, and wisdom to flow through your life. The sound of God is the audible lifestream that uplifts you and helps you open your heart to love and to God. The sound is similar to the vibrations created from molecules, but more so. When your inner awareness is attuned to the levels of God, you may be consciously aware of these vibrations or sounds. The light of God is the energy that makes up all of life.

You may already have heard the different sounds of God and not even realized what was happening. The first time I remember hearing the sound of God was when I was a child. My mom or dad would send me to bed and I would lay there terrified of some boogeyman coming out of my closet. As I lay in bed totally motionless with the covers over my head, I would hear this humming, similar to the sound of powerful electrical wires. The sound was comforting, but I didn't know what it was. Now when I hear sound, I realize it is Spirit's way of communicating to me, and it makes me more conscious of what is happening in the moment. Sound helps me gain more wisdom and clarity. If I had this knowledge of sound when I was a child, I could have been more of an active participant by consciously allowing it to fill my being. Having knowledge gives you choices of how to use that knowledge; and the more you are aware of how life works, the more fully and consciously you can participate in your life.

Physical Universe 🦋

Knowing there are many worlds of existence and many ways to experience reality may help you to participate more fully should you encounter sound and light or different universes in your dreams or contemplations. The universes are where Souls live, grow, and learn. These universes have their own qualities and governing laws.

First there is the physical universe. This is where you are now. The physical universe has laws of gravity and cause and effect, and material properties which include energy, space, and time. It is the most dense of all the universes. The term dense refers to how light and sound form physical creations. An example of this is that ice is more dense than steam. The energy that makes up steam is less dense than its counterpart of ice. The difference between the two creations is how dense or solid the molecules of energy are. (Remember this analogy as I describe the other universes.)

Any world of form, of any kind, is called a "lower" world, because it is less than pure Spirit. In these worlds you still need some kind of body for Soul to use so it can function in that particular vibration. (Vibrations, once again, are the movement of the light and sound.) Vibrations are simply energy. Any kind of body is made up of energy. On the physical level of existence, there is less light and sound apparent. Compared to the other universes, the life lessons on the physical are harder, but because of these life lessons, you have more opportunities to change your negative karma. The classical spiritual sound associated with this plane is thunder, though other sounds can be heard by your spiritual self. This is the world of the senses. The color most associated with this plane is green.

When I speak of the worlds of existence, I describe them in a general way, because everyone has a personal experience of a place. It is like describing a city you have visited to a friend who hasn't been there. You might speak in general terms about your experience of that place. When your friend visits there at another time, the experiences might be different, and your friend's description might differ from yours.

Neither one of you is wrong in your observations; you just have had different experiences of the same place. Both of you have been there, but the particular experience was different. Just look around this planet and see all the different cultures. This planet is a miniscule part of a whole physical universe. It would be nearly impossible for one person to describe fully all the aspects of life on this physical planet, or any of the other universes, because of the limitations of an individual's viewpoint and the enormity of the places involved.

Astral Universe ও

The next highest world is the astral. This universe has more light, sound, and freedom. It is bigger than the physical universe and the laws that govern it are different. The inhabitants of the astral universe can look like us, but their bodies are less dense and have more Spiritual light. Their vibrations of energy are finer, and they can move about freely by just thinking. This is the plane of emotion, the highest place most people reach by astral projection. The sound associated with this world is the roar of the sea, and its predominant color is pink.

Causal, Mental, and Etheric Universes 🕊

The next worlds, in succession, are the causal, mental, and etheric. When use I the words "higher" or "lower" in describing these worlds, understand they are linear descriptions. In this world of space and time, we think in terms of "up" and "down," "higher" and "lower." In truth, these different worlds exist simultaneously. We experience them when our consciousness is of a similar vibration. We can experience them even in this physical plane through our dreams or contemplations. I believe my dreams are real experiences, so when I dream or I am in contemplation and I see or hear the aspects of these different universes, I actively use this information to help me through problems here. For example, if I saw a pink color through a contemplation, that might be an indicator that something is bothering me or I need attention on some emotional issue. (Pink, remember, is the color of the astral plane and it corresponds with emotions.) Soul is always communicating with your human consciousness in ways you can understand. Becoming more conscious of your signposts helps you to unblock obstacles to your direct knowing of God and Spirit.

These next levels are also mixtures of Spirit and some kind of form. The color designated for the causal world is orange and the sound there is the tinkling of bells. The mental plane is blue and the sound is running water. The etheric, which is the highest world with some kind of form, has the predominant color purple and the sound of buzzing bees. All the worlds can have all colors and all sounds.

The upper worlds are larger and more spiritual, and they have less form and more Spirit. There is still some kind of body covering Soul, but the bodies are less dense and are made up of finer molecules. Each body has a unique vibrational rate, as we do here on Earth. In the higher worlds, the bodies get finer and finer and are more light-filled. They are closer to being pure Spirit. Having some kind of body indicates some form of duality, and duality is something less than the pure Soul experience. So our ultimate goal should be to evolve to the pure spiritual state. Since we have a body and we are here now, we need to work toward our ultimate goal with great care and respect for our human life. A necessary step in our evolution as Soul is being human and encountering and growing through our lessons. Ending our life sooner than our natural life span is a negative action, and we will have to return to face the karma we incurred because of our actions. We can never escape the lessons or karma we need to have in order to be our truest selves.

Duality or Polarity ❧

Duality or polarity is the way we learn in the lower worlds of God. Duality means something composed of contrary or opposite qualities. Let's take an example of duality that is found on Earth. To experience warmth, you must experience cold. To experience a positive, there must be a negative. To have a mountain, there must be a valley. The intrinsic nature of form is duality. When there is form, you cannot escape having opposites.

In the higher realms of God, in all the worlds "higher" than the etheric, there is no form, and so, no duality. You reside as pure Spirit: light, sound, and love. You no longer need a body. You are one with the light and sound of God, one with Spirit and love. The upper worlds are the pure worlds of light, sound, love, being, and knowing. They are impossible to describe with words, because words are of the lower universes. Words come from the mind, and Soul is above the mind.

In these worlds, you are no longer encumbered with karma. You have complete freedom. You take on and experience karma only when you are in the lower worlds. The worlds above the physical universe are what the Bible calls heaven. Heaven is not a place where people mill about in flowing robes, just having a good time. Actually, the Heavens are active states that are always changing and growing, just like on Earth. As Soul, you are always changing, learning, and growing, because God cannot be fully known.

God and Your Daily Life ❧

So how does this pertain to your daily life here and your potential happiness? If you don't have a goal or a destination in mind, then getting ahead or being in control of your life is greatly diminished or blocked altogether. We all want happiness. Most of us want peace, security, and joy, but most of the people I see in therapy and average people in the world today are unconscious about what life and living is all about. Knowing your goal gives you purpose and direction. You can ascertain what actions to take here and now to reach your destination only when you know what that destination is.

Most of the people on this planet are less than satisfied with their lives. Many feel powerless, and they don't know what to do to achieve more satisfaction with their lives. Think about it: if you don't know the rules of life, how can you participate fully?

If you continue to live only from the small consciousness of your mind, ego, and emotions, you will never experience the true greatness life has to offer. It is only when you get **beyond** the human state of consciousness that anything lasting comes into your life. The reality on Earth is that all things change. The **only** constant is change. So if you consistently put your energy into things of limited duration, no true joy can stay in your life. When you dedicate your life to the limitless reality of Spirit and God, true meaning and happiness can be yours, **now**, in this lifetime.

Let's put this idea to work. Most of us go to work, pay our bills, get married, have children, cry, laugh, overcome hardships, eat, sleep, and have fun. This will never change. It is not what you do that counts so much as where you focus your awareness and attention while you make these actions. Your focus creates your connection to God and develops your inner growth. Aspire to make your life actions in the name of God, not just for your human ego or for physical survival. When you come from this point of Spirit, you live each day eliminating negative karma, and your chances of creating new negative karma are greatly reduced. Your daily life becomes something very special indeed!

When you start the day dedicating your daily actions to God, you raise your vibrations and work with Him. When you dedicate your actions to Spirit, you allow Spirit to flow through you, positively affecting your daily life and your actions. You positively affect everything and everyone around you, whether anyone is aware of it or not.

You create negative karma only when you make actions based solely from your lower self, like the ego or bodily desires. That's not to say actions from your ego or physical self can't be positive. Generally when you come from your lower self, your actions are usually self-centered. You might not consider the whole of life, so the possibility of producing negative karma is greater when you come from the ego.

We are all part of God, so there is truly no separation between us and all of life. When you live from an enlightened awareness, you know all creatures are a part of God and thus part of you. Whatever you do to create value for yourself creates value for the whole of life. Also whatever you do to create value for others **without devaluing yourself** is also good for you.

Living from this higher state does not mean losing yourself in any way. It is **NOT** being a martyr. What it does mean is living in an individual way without impinging on others. It means living the happiest, most fulfilled life you can, while staying in harmony and purpose with God and Spirit by being yourself. This is accomplished through your daily actions. Your actions and energy become messengers for others, to help them know what life is about.

Martyrdom ❧

I was taught, as many of us were, that to be a "good" person meant you had to be a martyr. You never allowed yourself to love yourself fully. Everyone else's desires took precedence over your own well-being. Being a martyr means sacrificing self-esteem or desires for another person, even to the point of hurting one's own health or wellbeing. Martyrs, in my opinion, are victims!

I wanted very much to be a loving and evolved person. So I let people walk all over me, because I thought this was what being "loving" meant, negating the self. I ended up stuffing a lot of anger, and I didn't love myself. For years I had terribly low self-esteem, and I didn't allow myself to live in a healthy way. I became a victim under the guise of wanting to be a good person.

Think now, how can you love anyone, including God, if you don't love yourself? How can you let love into your being if you are a victim? This is what I came to terms with. I began to realize that truly being happy and loving God and all His creatures begins with self-love and self-respect.

Love Yourself ❧

One way you love yourself is by establishing your personal growth process and boundaries. You are the one who has to meet your needs and defend yourself from people trying to control you. You are in charge of your life! Each individual is unique, so the requirements for your life will be different than anyone else's.

Only when you love yourself can you truly know Spirit. Loving yourself sometimes means you may have to say "no" to others' requests. The more you give yourself what you need and base your actions on becoming a more aware and loving person, the more you will become connected to God. Spirit will then flow through you in a natural way to bring light, sound, and love to you and others around you. This is service, a blend of self-love and nurturing that allows Spirit to flow through you while you do what you need to do for your happiness and growth. Service is not a giving up the things you like to do. Service is an attitude, a state of being, while you do the things you love to do in your life.

Only when you love yourself and you do what is best for your life can you be a healthy vehicle for Spirit. Only then can you truly love others fully. Spirit does not ask you to deny yourself for others or to be a martyr. Spirit asks that you be all you can be and allow It to move through you to affect others in a non-invasive, noncontrolling way. You accomplish this when you first give yourself love and self-respect.

Observe the victims and martyrs you know. Do they bring light and love to anyone? Think of all the bright, happy, self-fulfilled people you know. Aren't they truly doing God's work by being happy? The energy of the victims and martyrs is negative, constrictive, and dark; the energy of a self-loving person is expansive, lighter, and brighter. When people who love themselves declare themselves to be vehicles for God, all their actions take on a greater effectiveness, because they send light and love to others from Soul. Sometimes, by their presence, others are brought closer to God. What counts in spiritual growth is the consciousness of the individual, how close and connected one is to Spirit in daily life.

Treating yourself with love and respect is your first link with God. You then can affect other people without interfering with their free will. **This is an important point!** Linking up with Spirit and God does not entail forcing or controlling others to think or be any certain way. Think of yourself as an open tube. Allow the light and sound of God to flow through you, while being detached to the effect it may have on others. Be unconcerned about whether others are open to receive Spirit, because you know it is not up to you to control others' growth.

Contemplation vs. Meditation or Prayer ⁊⬤

So how do you bring Spirit and God into your life? You can do this by a process called contemplation, which brings the love, light, and sound of Spirit and God into every part of yourself. Contemplation is not like prayer or meditation, which can be passive ways of trying to connect with God. Contemplation is active. In contemplation, you are actively uniting with Spirit.

A client in a seminar I was conducting described beautifully the difference between the three practices. She said prayer is the vehicle one uses to talk to God, meditation is when you are listening for Him and contemplation was your union with God, Spirit, or yourself as Soul.

When you go above your emotions and your mind as Soul in contemplations, changes in your life occur faster and they are more comprehensive than with meditation or prayer. With contemplation, you link up with yourself as Soul. Contemplation is a spiritual exercise in which you actively seek out higher awareness. You are not passively waiting for it to come to you.

Soul is the life force of being human. So when you contact Soul in your daily life, as with contemplations, it affects all parts of you in a most positive way. We each have parts that make us human. They are, in simple terms, the Soul, the conscious and unconscious mind, the emotional self, and the physical self. These are real bodies within your physical body. When Soul leaves, your physical body dies. The growth and connection you make with Spirit and Soul during contemplation has an effect on your physical life now and after death. This is the greatest growth you can have. Contemplation is a most powerful tool for anyone to use to connect with Spirit or God.

Contemplation brings us into union with love and the twin aspects of sound and light. It helps open our hearts to love. I will emphasize the twin aspects of sound and light here because I have devoted a whole chapter to the subject of love.

Sound and light are the basic purifying elements of God and Spirit. There is sound and light on every plane of existence, and the purely Spiritual planes are only filled with this sound and light. The closer you get to God, the brighter the light is and the more beautiful the sound.

Light on Earth is experienced most commonly through spiritual practices. It is seen by your inner eye, which sometimes is called your third eye. It is a tool for your Soul to see light and hear sound while in the physical body. Know, as your awareness grows, you may hear sound and see light outside of your formal contemplations. The more you expand your awareness through contemplation, the more you will connect and unify with sound and light.

90

These aspects of God help cleanse you of negativity and open you to Spirit. The changes usually start at the level of Soul and filter to the rest of you.

The light of Spirit can come in all colors. Sometimes the light of Spirit is seen as stars, like specks that sparkle, flashes, or larger pointed stars. Many times the stars are blue. It doesn't matter what form or color the light takes, just know the light is of Spirit. If and when you see it, it is a sign your consciousness is being uplifted for a deeper understanding of life and helping you know on some level what you need in order to grow.

Of the two aspects of God, sound—the movement or speed of the vibrations of energy on any certain level of existence—is the most important. You see light and hear sounds according to the levels of your consciousness. As you grow in awareness, your ability to hear the different sounds of Spirit and see the different light grows. Sound is important because it helps balance your spiritual growth in the physical body. Sound is an indication you are making changes, and it has many different functions. One function is that it is the pure God energy moving through you, rearranging aspects of your being that are not in alignment with Spirit.

Also if you grow too fast in spiritual consciousness, you may feel unbalanced emotionally, mentally, or physically. One of the properties of sound is to help you balance your whole self while you are going through your growth and changes. It monitors your growth.

The many sounds you can hear in contemplation are like those on the physical plane: thunder, wind, bells, a single note of the flute, violins, and humming like that of electrical wires, to name just a few. You will know they are spiritual when you hear them unconnected to what would normally cause them. For example, if you hear thunder when there is no storm in sight or hear the buzzing of bees

91

when you know there are none around, you can assume you have heard Sound.

Sound is God's way of communicating to you. The sound of God has always been. Sound was even mentioned in the Bible on two occasions; when the apostles heard the rushing of the wind at the last supper, and when it mentioned, "In the beginning there was the Word." Few religions teach about sound, or if they do mention it, most don't know how to contact it. This is why it is so fundamental to have a daily spiritual practice, so you can get connected again to your roots. Contemplations help you to connect to the sound and light of God.

Steps in Creating a Contemplation ❧

EXERCISE

Choosing a High Vibratory Word

A very powerful way to start a contemplation is to start out singing or chanting, if you will, the oldest name for God, and that is "HU." "HU" represents the love God has for you as Soul. Singing "HU" (pronounced like the name Hugh) affects your vibrations by raising them. When you raise your vibrations, you go above your mind and emotions and connect directly with Spirit to a higher state of awareness. It is very similar to climbing to higher ground to find your way if your are lost. Your perspective from the higher ground is broader and more accurate. This is what you do when you chant any high vibratory word. You set up your energy to accept and understand Spirit and God from a higher perspective.

Some other words you can sing are "God," "Aum," "Wah Z," or "Sugmad," which is another ancient name for God. Choose one that feels right to you. Then close your eyes, sit comfortably with your feet flat on the floor and focus gently on the place between your eyes. As you exhale, sing the word of your choice. Elongate the words. "HU" sounds like "Huuuuuuuuu." "Wah Z" sounds like this, "Waaaahhhh Zeeeeee," and so forth.

Do this for 10 to 20 minutes. You may see a blue light or hear some of the sounds I've mentioned. Whatever happens, know you are linking up with your Soul and with Spirit, and you are safe and protected. Sometimes it may seem like nothing is happening, but the very use of the word "HU" (or any of the other words) will raise your vibrations and bring you spiritual protection and growth in every aspect of your life. This is especially true when you consistently incorporate contemplations in your life. 🐾

EXERCISE

Prepare with Feeling

After you have sung your word for 10 to 20 minutes, use your imagination to increase the growth and your Spiritual connection with Spirit. Your imagination is a powerful tool to help you grow and link yourself as Soul. If you can't clearly visualize, that's okay. The more you do it, the better you will get. The key is relaxing and trusting your higher self. Also, if I had to choose between feeling or seeing pictures, I'd pick feeling. Visualization may be your road map to change, but your feelings are the gas that runs your car. Without the gas, you get nowhere. Just remember a time when you REALLY wanted something and got it. You got it because of the emotions behind your desire.

In any contemplation it is VERY important to begin with a feeling of love. Love is the golden key to changing yourself and bringing you closer to knowing God in this lifetime. If love is hard for you to bring up or feel, try to remember a time when you were in love and how it felt when it was positive. The more you bring up and fill your heart with love during your contemplations, the more love comes into your life and it connects you with God, for God is love. ❧

Connecting to Spirit and God is experiential. As with anything else, the more you practice, the better you get. So if you have never experienced a spiritual contemplation, give yourself lots of time and acceptance. Experiment honestly with it for a period of time, a month or two, and then compare how you feel and how you experience life after that time.

Here are some suggestions of what to do after you've sung your chosen word for a few minutes. Just remember you are in charge of your life. You have the freedom to create your contemplations anyway you want, so they are pertinent to you. Feel free to use these visualizations, or not.

Creative Imagination on Inner Child

Some of these visualizations have helped me work with my inner child and helped me work through negative feelings about myself. When I speak of my inner child, I am referring to my emotional self. Most of us have a wounded emotional self which is stuck in childhood. I've visualized my adult self re-educating my inner child to help her love herself more and help her overcome fears that were brought on by living in a dysfunctional family in this life or from some other life of mine. For example, imagine your adult self back in time communicating to your inner child. Pick different scenarios in your life when you felt unsafe, shamed, unloved, or angry. Be there for your inner child. If your inner child has felt unloved, change the situation so your inner child feels loved unconditionally. If your father or mother abused you, give your inner child a chance to safely express its anger, and then give it new, loving, understanding role models, etc. This is a process, and as you heal one aspect of your inner child, you strengthen yourself to feel and heal more issues. It doesn't matter what the problems are or where the problems began. Always remember the power to change anything in your life is in the present moment, the endless now. ❧

EXERCISE

Spiritual School

One other visualization you could try would be to see yourself in a higher world of beautiful light. Imagine yourself learning life, love, and wisdom at Spiritual schools, taught by Spiritual masters. Your imagination is real and extremely powerful. When you are in a contemplation and imagining you are some-place or trying to heal something in your life, know what you imagine really does happen on some level in your being. Remember, imagination is one of the func-tions of a higher part of yourself. It is a powerful aspect to creating. You have to imagine something before it becomes real on the physical plane. For exam-ple, an architect imagines a house before drawing the plans. What came first was the visualization. ∂

EXERCISE

Receiving Divine Help

During another contemplation, after you have sung your word, visualize yourself standing in a beautiful river and see a Spiritually enlightened being (Christ, Buddha, or a Guardian Angel) next to you. Next, see yourself giving that Spiritual being all your anger, fears, questions, and anything else you want to get rid of. Feel the love of Spirit coming from the Being and know you are being helped. See the Spiritual being accepting what you want to get rid of in a basket and dumping it down the river of Spirit. Feel yourself cleansed and filled with love, light, and the sound of God. ∂

Spiritual Travel

Another exercise to try, after you have sung your chosen word, could be to imagine yourself leaving your physical body. See yourself standing outside your physical body and looking at it. Imagine the white light around it and know you are safe. This process, when actualized in you leaving your body, is sometimes called astral projection. With astral projection you are using your astral body and it is limited to the realm of the astral plane. With this exercise you are expanding the possibilities of what is real, and it helps you realize you are not your body. Astral projection is really a part of "Soul travel," a higher form of spiritual travel, taught by Eckankar. With Soul travel you are expanding your consciousness as Soul towards God and have the freedom to visit the higher worlds, sometimes even the worlds of pure Spirit. Most everyone leaves the body in some way every night while sleeping, but most people have no conscious recollection of the experience. When you are asking to be your highest self in this life, you are asking to be fully conscious of all your experiences. This is living from total awareness.

After you have visualized yourself outside your body, then see a Spiritual being and the spiritual part of you talking together. Visualize both yourself and the higher being as bodies of sparkling light, like thousands of little stars. See that being teach you what you need to learn now to help you in your higher growth. ❧

As you can see, contemplations can be limitless. The key to reaching the highest states of being is to do these daily with love. State before you start your day that your actions are a vehicle for Spirit and God. With that, your life will evolve in love and higher awareness. You will realize why you are here. Everything in your life, your every action, takes on the qualities of mercy and love. You then become the messenger of God, even while you sleep.

Dreams 🍂

As you grow in Spirit, you also grow in awareness of the realities you can experience. Your dreams might become more lucid. You may feel like you are experiencing the things depicted in your dreams, and they may seem clearer in content. Dreams are a very real part of your life. Dreams are a way for Spirit to communicate to you. Some dreams are from a purely to-teach-you basis, where Soul is getting information for Its growth. Other dreams are prophetic in nature. Sometimes you may learn things in your dreams that help your daily life go a little smoother. Other dreams are true Soul journeys out of the body to other inner worlds you will remember as dreams. As you focus on your dreams more, you will begin to know what they are trying to convey to you. Keeping a dream journal helps you to focus on your dreams and helps you to remember them. As you grow toward God, your consciousness is awakened both in the day and night with your dreams. When this happens, you can use every moment to grow and learn.

Waking Dreams 🍂

Spirit talks to you in the daytime by waking dreams or the synchronicity of events. The more you are tuned to

Spirit, the more you understand the message. Let me give you some examples of waking dreams.

For years I have tried to overcome my fears of being alone and vulnerable. Being on my own at 15 left a lot of pain and hurt in my life and an underlying belief I was alone in life without protection. This has affected almost every aspect of my life. I found it very hard to feel secure and safe. Little snags that come up in my daily life can appear as very real threats to my security. Let me give you an example.

One day, my car battery died unexpectedly. Then the very same day I got a speeding ticket. The next week, my car had a flat tire at night (which particularly annoyed me). I left it in the shop all the next day so the tire could be repaired. They didn't finish my car in time for me to take it home that day, so I told them to lock it up and leave it in their parking lot and I'd pick it up after I finished with my clients. After I saw my last client, I got a ride to the garage and I discovered that they had locked my car in for the night!

These occurrences were a waking dream for me. I felt the spiritual message in the situations, especially since they all occurred fairly close together. In all those situations, someone was right there to help me very quickly. Even with the flat tire, a motorist called the police and they came within five minutes. This particularly had an impact on me because in my past I had felt so alone and afraid, and without transportation, I had felt particularly vulnerable. Spirit was telling me I am protected.

During each situation I silently chanted "HU" to myself and made actions to remedy the situation the best I could. There was always a ride and I never lost any work. I now have a deeper trust in the protection of Spirit, and I know trust is necessary for my further growth as Soul.

What seemed like annoyances were really Spirit giving me valuable lessons and support.

This is just one example of a waking dream. Another happened when I was having difficulty finding a name for this book. Nothing seemed right. When I threw out suggestions, no one liked any name I created. When I was on a little vacation I did a lot of contemplations for guidance on the title of my book. On the way home the part of title just flashed into my head, "Advanced Perceptions of Living." This is also the name of my company and has been for several years. When I asked my friends how they liked this name the response was only positive. My waking dream about this happened the next day when a new client came into my office. On the door is the name of my company, "Advanced Perceptions," and she pointed to my company name and said she really liked it. No client before or since has ever done that. I felt her response was a powerful, confirming message from Spirit. I absolutely felt "Advanced Perceptions" would be in the title, but part of me did not feel totally comfortable with it. So I kept an open heart for any guidance. Months later I was in a class and one of the participants was talking and in her conversation she said, "Soul never sleeps."

Immediately and without conscious thought I said out loud, "Soul Never Sleeps is a great name for a book." The next day that phrase haunted me until I acknowledged that this should be the prominent title of my book. After I acknowledged it, a great sense of peace came over me. Both occurrences were waking dreams, Spirit's way of teaching.

Waking dreams also can be as simple as several people telling you to go to a certain kind of doctor when you have been asking Spirit for guidance about your health. Spirit is always talking to you. You just have to be aware enough to listen. The more aware you are, the more you notice Spirit speaking to you in your daily life, helping you to learn and grow.

In finding God, you have free will. You can be the victim and wait for Him to contact you. Or you can take an active role in your reaching God. I believe taking an active role is the only way anyone reaches God and His love, in life or death. You have to want to reach Him, and know He is always there for you when you are ready to connect with Him.

Relationships

The robin calls
to his mate,
his song is one only she
can relate.

Their dance begins
again . . .
song to song
flight entwined.

Soaring ever higher
yet at times just perched,
overlooking the world
together—yet apart.

Sharing is their dance
their flight of life,
one encouraging the other
to the endless reaches
of their possibilities. ❧

Chapter 5

Relationships

Something you cannot escape from in this life is relationships. Relationships can run the gamut from painful to blissful, and they can create much confusion. If you try to escape having relationships, you still have the relationship with yourself to deal with. Even a hermit, isolated on a desert island, still has to deal with himself. In this chapter, we'll simplify the confusion that comes from relating with others, ourselves, and life. We'll discuss the more day-to-day workings of being human.

Your Relationship with Yourself ❧

The most important relationship you will ever have is the one with yourself. Until you are clear about your relationship with yourself, no other relationship in your life will be clear. And consequently, you will be at a loss on how to relate to others in worthwhile ways.

Always keep in mind that your true essence is Soul, and all relationships in life are tools to help bring you to this understanding and awareness. Attaining unconditional love and understanding of yourself is a vital requirement to this awareness. Many people have no idea what will make them happy. Often, they search for identity and happiness through other people or by acquiring things. Many people never really know themselves. Knowing yourself and knowing your needs as an individual are crucial to your day-to-day and overall happiness. This is true if your desire for your life is a higher awareness of yourself as Soul or not.

You will never find true happiness outside yourself! If this sounds like a strong statement to you, good. You are the only one who can make yourself happy, and the faster you come to this realization the quicker you can have the happiness you seek. It's imperative for you to fulfill your own needs as an individual to make this happen. You do this by letting yourself know what you need, then giving yourself the things that are essential in embracing your happiness, regardless if those things are physical, mental, emotional, or spiritual.

A Healthy Self 🍂

There are many opinions about what constitutes a healthy self. My definition of a healthy self is someone who consistently makes loving actions with his or her life. A healthy self is someone who can love himself or herself for being, not just for his or her accomplishments. A healthy relationship with yourself involves allowing yourself to get your needs met on every level. This covers the spiritual, mental, emotional, and physical parts of yourself. Healthy individuals know only they can make their lives happy. It's treating yourself as you would treat another person when you are deeply in love. It's respecting yourself enough to say "no" when you really want to say "no" and not feel guilty. It's knowing that other people's feelings are not more important than yours.

These are just some fundamental aspects to a healthy relationship with yourself. Basically, no one can change anything in your life for you...but you.

Co-Dependence 🍂

The relationship buzzword of the '90s is co-dependence. People who are co-dependent compensate for their bad feelings about themselves by seeking approval and worth through other people, things, or accomplishments. They try to get love and approval outside of themselves. This may manifest by their taking on the roles of either super-responsible nurturers or victims. They basically let themselves be abused. The abuse they allow into their lives can be emotional, mental, or physical. They believe (consciously or unconsciously) they are powerless to change the circumstances in their life. They are allowing themselves to be victims. Victims are people who are not allowing themselves to get their needs met. They sabotage their control and personal power in their life. A victim can be either the ultra-responsible, indispensable nurturer or the martyr. I tell my clients there really are only two kinds of people: victims and people who give themselves permission to use their personal power to create what they want in life.

Whether you are aware of it or not, you might still be making choices and living your life in response to a negative inner image. If this is true, that inner belief is coloring everything in your life. Until you change that negative inner belief, you may try to compensate for your negative feelings about yourself by living co-dependently, as a martyr or a dysfunctional nurturer.

Dysfunctional Nurturer 🐚

The super nurturer, the overly responsible person, is trying unconsciously to get love and to feel whole. The way they go about this is by overstepping their boundaries with others. Unconsciously they feel if they do for others, then they are good people and they can love themselves. They tend to overstep other people's boundaries, trying to control others by making choices for them, manipulating, or overextending themselves in other people's lives. They do much more than is healthy to do for others. They usually cover up their own feelings to protect another. A typical belief or response of a dysfunctional nurturer would be to withhold opinions or suppress anger because, "It would hurt the other person too much if I told them I was angry," or "If they truly knew how I felt it would hurt them too much."

Dysfunctional nurturers take the responsibility for other people's feelings and responses. In doing so, they negate themselves. This is not living honestly. Withholding of necessary communication and feelings or trying to second guess and protect others from their feelings does not create healthy ground for honest self-growth or self-worth.

More...Martyr ❧

Martyrs, on the other hand, do not take responsibility for their lives. They blame the environment, circumstances, or other people for their lack of a happy life. They do not want to take responsibility for what they have created. These people usually have a hard time standing up for themselves and they allow others to step all over them. Martyrs hardly ever allow themselves to do what they truly want to do. They "sacrifice" their happiness and needs for others even when it is detrimental to their overall well-being and happiness.

If your inner martyr or dysfunctional nurturer is letting you be abused, by your own actions or by the actions of others, you are not uplifting or loving yourself. This is not the way to a healthy self. You can even play both roles. Either way, your relationship with yourself is one of degradation, and degradation is not the way to get the inner love and peace you so dearly want. Remember, even if you didn't know it at the time, you created this role, so you have the power to change it. To change your role in life, you must come to realize how you are living your life. This realization is your first step to a truly healthy relationship with yourself.

Unconditional Love 🕊

You need to love yourself unconditionally! It is imperative to understand this for your general happiness and higher ways of being. It is that simple and that profound!

Too many of us have grown up with the belief that in order to be good, we have to deny our own needs. This simply is not true. Each person has the **spiritual right** to be an individual and to do what is best. My life is different than yours and your life is different from anyone else's. Since our lessons are different, our needs are different. Remembering this is crucial to your health and happiness. If you are causing no harm to others and not interfering with or trying to control other people's lives or space, then doing whatever you need to do for your happiness is not only correct, but necessary and vital for your personal and spiritual growth.

To attain unconditional love, happiness, and spiritual advancement, inner shame from your childhood or from other traumatic happenings in your life needs to be healed. You need to understand deeply that you are worthwhile as a person, just for being part of God. Fully understanding how you have been living is crucial to changing the old patterns that are preventing you from creating your life to be the way you want it to be. Probably you will have to learn new ways of living your daily life.

For example, if you tend to want to "fix" people, understand that other people have lessons to learn and the right to fix themselves or not. If you tend to live your life as a victim, you have to realize it is up to you to take charge of your life before you can be happy.

Healing Yourself First ❧

True happiness and self-love only can be achieved when you put your emphasis toward healing your own self first. Co-dependent people try to be more complete through relating and doing for others while neglecting themselves. They feel if they do this or that for someone, then the other person will love them, and if another person loves them and approves of them, then they feel worthwhile. Most people are unconscious of this scenario. People who are co-dependent tend to feel and act on their inner belief that other people's feelings and needs are more important than their own. Their self-worth is fragile and linked with outside approval. Some people find themselves doing almost anything for that approval, because approval equals love and worth to the dysfunctional person. When you live with the belief that others are more valuable than you, or if you lose your individuality and self in order to get love and approval, then you deny yourself love and respect. All your relationships, including the one with yourself, get out of balance, and you lose love or never attain the love you so fervently seek.

Let me give you an example of what I mean. Since I came from a dysfunctional family, my opinion and deep feelings of myself were ones of shame. Inside I felt worthless. I did not give myself permission to be treated with respect, nor did I give myself many words of praise or love. I did not approve of myself. When I was on my own for the first couple of years, my bad feelings about myself peaked. I allowed myself to be abused physically by men, and financially I was just making it. I didn't feel good enough about myself to stop others from overstepping my boundaries. Because I didn't love myself, how could others? I always felt I didn't count and my feelings were unimportant. I was trying to get love and self-worth by being a doormat and a victim. I so desperately wanted love that I let myself lose my individuality and self-respect. At the time I was totally unconscious of this.

I remember one particular relationship when I was in my early twenties. The man in my life was verbally, emotionally, and physically abusive. There was nothing positive in this relationship. He was even mean to my cat! I stayed with him even though I got nothing but negativity. I felt I had no choice. I was desperate for love. But was this love? I know now it wasn't. At that time in my life, desperate for approval and love and empty inside, I allowed myself to be treated badly.

I remember that something clicked inside me one night when I was coming home from work. I realized I was allowing this abuse to happen. It wasn't him so much abusing me as I was giving my permission to be abused. With this realization, I felt liberated. From that night on I took steps to free myself from this abuse and I left. This was a lesson I have never forgotten. I attracted this man into my life because I hated myself and I only had myself to blame. I once again made myself the victim and created my own hell!

Unconsciously I thought if I did enough for others or for him, then I'd be worthy of love. I had it backwards. Now I know that if I raise myself up and truly love all parts of myself first, I will then attract to me all the respect, goodness, and love I deserve. We all deserve limitless supplies of love and all that is positive, and I always want to be a fully-functioning, happy, love-filled person.

For you to create and keep the love and the positive things in your life, it is necessary for you to know the mechanics of how your inner beliefs draw corresponding experiences to you.

Like Attracts Like ❧

You are energy vibrating at a certain rate. Your thoughts, emotions, and actions influence and create your vibrational rate. Your body is composed of cells and atoms. Scientists know there are even smaller particles than these and all particles of energy vibrate. In reality you are just vibrating energy! Your thoughts and feelings are also energy. This energy comes in a myriad of forms and densities. Like attracts like. You attract circumstances and relationships to you on the basis of your vibrational rate.

Physical objects, emotions, and thoughts vibrate at different rates. Though it seems like there is a separation between the physical, emotional, and mental parts of life, in reality all are ever-moving energy. What makes them look separate is that everything vibrates at different rates of speed, creating different densities, such as gases and solids, thoughts and emotions.

All energy, all of us, is part of Spirit. Spirit makes up all of what we think of as reality. Different things, such as plants, animals, and humans, have different consciousness or awareness of life, and they also have different rates of vibration. Your vibrational rate is your magnet. Your whole essence of being is vibrating and attracting, or "magnetizing," situations to yourself that reflect the total you. So if your total being vibrates with worthlessness, then you will attract or "magnetize" to you people and circumstances that reflect these particular sets of vibrations. It is the same with self-love.

In my past, I held the belief that men were not there for me or would treat me unkindly. I came to this belief because of my relationships with my brothers and my father. When I started to date, I attracted self-centered, uncaring, and, in some cases, abusive men. I was vibrating from the state of worthlessness. As I started to change my relationship with myself, I saw that the men I attracted were kinder and nicer. Changing the relationship with myself changed my vibrational rate; consequently, changing the situations and people I attracted into my life.

Changing Your Outer Environment ❧

Your relationship with yourself is the key to changing your relationships with everyone else in your life. Also, the other people in your life can be mirrors reflecting back to you what you need to change in your own life. Your interactions with other people also tell you what you need to change within your own self. For example, if you are being victimized by co-workers or your family, then look inside yourself to see what you need to change. If someone treats you in a way that you don't like, examine your relationship with yourself. If you have been attracting abuse, change within yourself the beliefs or emotional issues that created this in your life. When you have, you will then find that either the abusive person or persons will treat you better, they will leave your life, or you will leave theirs.

When you change, your environment has to change. This change in your environment has to happen because as you change your consciousness, you change your vibrations. Changing your consciousness changes your level of awareness or how "awake" you are living your life. As you may have already gathered, life can be lived in a limited, fundamental, survival mode, or in total realization that you are a Spiritual being with a definite purpose for living.

Your outer environment then, including the people in your life, is a reflection of all that is you. This is an absolute spiritual principle. To change the way someone treats you, change yourself. Then you will see a change in the people or circumstances around you.

I see changes in my clients and how they relate to life

113

all the time. Often people come into therapy when they have been living as victims. Maybe people at work or at home are always picking on them or yelling at them. When people allow this kind of abuse in their life, they are not standing up for themselves or defending their personal space and boundaries. As a therapist I know they must feel unworthy. Once they start treating themselves better, loving themselves, and feeling their inner worth, they start to stand up for themselves, and their environment changes. They see for themselves that the other abusive people change or move on.

Creating Your Reality: An Example ❧

One client, whom I'll name Mary, made major changes in her life when she started to realize and live these new understandings. Mary had been in one form of counseling or another for seven years before she came to my office. She had many health problems and felt totally powerless in her life. Her self-esteem was very low. I saw her only eight times before she moved out of state. Mary had a deep desire to grow, which is absolutely necessary to achieve any change. She worked very hard with the principles I taught her. In that short time we worked on her emotional, mental, and Spiritual selves.

Mary was brought up with very strong beliefs that she was a powerless victim and her body could never heal. She was surrounded by people who constantly invalidated her. Even in the different group therapies she attended, the people there helped to reinforce helplessness, victimhood, and powerlessness. She was never told or made aware she could change her view of life to a more empowering one.

I started to help her understand the concepts of creating her own reality. In all her years of therapy, she never had anyone ask her how she felt! So we worked with her inner child and her emotional self, making it safe for her to feel and process her unconscious anger. Each session I saw a change in her. As she tried on these new concepts, her life started to change. She started to stand up for herself and say "no" to people who were overstepping her boundaries. She released old, negative, limiting relationships and started to attract more positive people. She started to rely on her own self, to nurture herself and get her needs met. This was something she didn't know she could do before! As her unconscious beliefs started to change, she began to see her health problems as temporary and fixable, instead of a way of life. She had an eating disorder and it went away. Her zest for life and energy increased. She was tremendously excited about living life from the higher spiritual consciousness because she felt, for the first time, a sense of purpose in living.

Mary is a perfect example of how you change your environment by changing yourself! As her inner beliefs changed, her awareness of life and how she reacted to it changed. This in turn changed her vibrational level, attracting people and situations that reflected this new consciousness. She started to look at life as her teacher, instead of something to just muddle through. Relationships with ourselves and others are always teaching us, if we just open our hearts to ask for the message.

The exercises in the chapters, "Love" and "Balance," should start you on your way to having better feelings about yourself. Allow yourself every vehicle to help you achieve the self-love that you may need, whether it's therapy, group counseling, or getting in touch with your spiritual self.

Spirit has put all the tools you need within your grasp. At different times you may need different tools. The key to growth and change is allowing yourself what you need in the present moment. Love yourself enough to be flexible and listen to your inner self. Remember, growth and happiness are ongoing. Your inner growth and expanding happiness require your consistent actions.

Karmic Relationships ❧

Have you ever had the experience or feeling that you have known someone before and wondered why you felt that way? More than likely, you knew that person in a previous life. You might be in a relationship together now to learn from each other or heal old wounds. This is called a karmic relationship.

The more loving or spiritual you were together in the past, the closer you may feel toward that individual now. Also, he or she may be in your life because one of you may need to make of some kind of "restitution." Or you may be together to help each other grow spiritually and to heal the actions of your past. Try to look at your relationships with all the people in your life as vehicles for your growth.

Some of these karmic relationships can be intense. They can last any length of time, from a day to years. The more you let Spirit guide you, the faster you grow. Your lessons are then speeded up. Most lessons require relating to other people whether they were known to you in past lives or not. The person who consistently separates herself or himself from other people usually has slower growth than someone who relates to others.

What is absolutely necessary for your growth is your **willingness** to confront yourself honestly, so Spirit can flow through you to affect you and others. If you refuse to relate to others or refuse to be honest with yourself in confronting what you need to do to change, then the flow of Spirit and love is blocked. You can only grow so far. The very acts of confronting yourself and working through what you find changes your consciousness. Take the example of Mary, she grew quickly because she was willing to boldly confront within herself the reasons her life was the way it was.

Love Requires Action ❧

Relationships are active when you help yourself and others at the same time. LOVING IS AN ACTIVE STATE! The higher your awareness, the more love you let flow through you and flow to others. Relationships help you become a more loving being.

As you grow spiritually, your lessons with different loved ones may manifest more quickly. At first this may cause conflict or disharmony. This disharmony is just a refinement of your vibrations as you evolve spiritually. It is similar to eating healthy foods or fasting when your previous diet has been really filled with unhealthy foods. Once you start refining your diet with healthier foods you may feel worse before you feel better. This is because the body now has the fuel to "houseclean" all the toxins out of your body. So as you both grow spiritually, you probably will "clean" a little negative karma together.

People who are very close to each other usually have more lessons to learn from their relationship. In the instance of people who are married, the lessons from the relationship can be far more intense and far reaching than those with casual acquaintances. The same holds true for family and good friends. Many times, when the spiritual lessons are over, people might go on to new lessons with other people. As you grow, you may see different people come and go in your life, including spouses.

Growth Through Relationships 🙠

In my own life, a relationship that has meant tremendous growth for me is my relationship with a man named Paul. I met him at a seminar in Elmira, New York while we were both going through divorces.

When I first met him I was not immediately attracted to him. But as the seminar progressed I talked more with him, and I felt very drawn to him. In my dreams I experienced his energy and presence. Later I found out he experienced the same with me.

By the end of the seminar we were inseparable, and I was sad that the seminar was ending. He decided to drive me to the airport so I could catch my flight home to Atlanta, and then he was going to drive home to Toronto. On the way to the airport, he spontaneously decided to fly with me to Atlanta! Well, I think it's every women's fantasy to be pursued, and I remember I was quite flattered by his affection and attention.

In Atlanta, we spent four days together. Since I hadn't planned this to happen, I still had clients to see. But many cancelled during his stay, which gave us even more time together. During his stay we had a great time and grew extremely close very quickly.

Paul had to go back to Toronto after a few days, and since we met right before Christmas, I decided to take my Christmas break with him in Canada. So I spent ten great days in Toronto with him, and by the end of the ten days he asked me to marry him, and I said "yes."

We both knew it was very fast but our connection was extremely deep. I had never before connected this way with anyone else. Immediately, we started to plan to live together. We ended up choosing Atlanta as a place to live, because Canadian law doesn't allow people who aren't medical doctors to practice hypnotherapy, and Paul, an actor, could make a living in the States.

From January to April, we both tried to keep communicating and seeing each other as much as we could. We were flying back and forth and creating a lot of costly phone bills, and he wrote me the most beautiful letters!

When he came down to Atlanta in April, we found a beautiful house and bought it together. He moved in that month and our intense life lessons began, because our deep love for each other had opened the way for our healing to surface. Both of us had come from dysfunctional homes, and we were co-dependent in our former marriages. When we were living together, we were aware of these facts and worked at eliminating this behavior from our relationship.

We wanted to have a marriage free of co-dependency, and to love each other in the unconditional way that makes it safe to be totally ourselves. We both wanted to be complete and happy individuals who didn't NEED the other to be happy within ourselves, but who wanted to be with each other to share our wholeness.

Both of us were concerned with growth, and we tried to always incorporate our spirituality into our daily lives. Our love and connection with Spirit opened the door for incredible healing for both of us, but not in the way you might expect. What happened next was that Paul found out his father had cancer. My father also was dying of cancer, and our fathers died about a month apart. We delayed our marriage, we rationalized, because of our fathers' deaths. Really, we were finding more lessons in our deeper selves that would require time apart.

In only a year, we both went through incredible losses. Paul got divorced and sold the farm which was his life's dream. He left his country and his father died. I got divorced, my cat—my dear friend of 17 years—died, and my father died. These were just the outer changes. Internally we both were letting go of long-held negative beliefs about our own worth. We both grew a lot in knowing about love and its power to heal.

With Paul's love I was able to feel more secure and self-loving. From this change in myself, I was able to give love to others without losing myself. Though I knew I still had to let go of more layers of deeper internal fears and any remaining tendencies to co-dependency. Through our love, Paul felt safe enough to be more of himself and he went through a lot of tough development and decision-making. He knew he loved me, and yet he also knew he had never given himself the space he needed for his own development.

For the next few months it was very difficult. Paul was trying to decide if he should marry me or go back to Canada. I was feeling his indecision, and I tried not to force him to stay. I believe that when you love someone you shouldn't manipulate them to do what you want them to do. Still, it was extremely hard for me to come to terms with Paul's indecision.

Paul decided to go back to Canada and for us not to marry. I was devastated at first. It has taken a lot for me to get over that, but the changes in me, my growth, and inner peace about myself have been tremendous. We both were better off knowing each other than if we never met.

Spirit and Healing ❧

I believe that Spirit put us together to help each other heal our past internalized issues. Our relationship was intense, loving, and growth-oriented. Our relationship was very deep and healing on all levels. I had, over the year we were together, many dreams about us. These dreams represented our growth together and revealed to me former lives I had spent with him. Through these dreams, I realized I had known Paul in many, many lifetimes and they went way, way back in time.

I grew lifetimes through knowing and loving Paul. Because we didn't marry doesn't mean our relationship was a failure. We grew in our capacity to love. By loving ourselves and sharing a deep love through each other, the relationship was truly a success!

Levels of Relating ❧

Relationships can be dealt with on many levels. It is up to you to choose how to deal with people in your life. You can approach life and people in your life from a limited or limitless viewpoint. When you put Spirit first in your life, you will relate to people in the most effective way for your and others' total growth. When you live life in this way, you are coming from a limitless, higher purpose for living.

The only unchanging thing in life is Spirit, which is love. The more you love yourself and others, the more you will get in touch with that which is changeless, that which is real. The foremost relationship to nurture is the one with yourself, Spirit, and God.

I try to live my life integrating my spiritual self with all the rest of me. All the people that come into my life, from the most significant to the most incidental, are in my life for a purpose. I am choosing to learn from all people.

In my romantic relationships, I have seen myself change from relating to men on merely a physical level to a more complete level, like my relationship with Paul. As I focus on spiritual growth and view other people as Souls needing particular experiences in their journeys of growth, my life and my relationships have gotten better and more rewarding.

Releasing Attachments ❧

My co-dependency is dropping away faster now, because I realize that I am not responsible for other people's happiness or growth. Previously I might have tried to force advice or help people because I thought it was for their own good. I now realize that maybe they need a particular lesson (which might entail some suffering) for their spiritual growth. I am getting better at not forcing my views on others. If I offer advice now and it isn't taken, I can understand others are entitled to their own opinions.

It's not that I don't care about people. (I wouldn't be writing this book if I didn't care.) It's that I am now trying to release attachments regarding what my ego might think is better for someone else's life. When I live in this way, I not only grow and get what's best for me, but I let others grow in the way that is perfect for them as their true selves as Soul.

Sometimes living your life for the good of all means separation. Other times it might mean you will be with someone for the rest of your life. Spirit knows what's best, not your ego. If I had held tightly to Paul and manipulated him to stay because I thought it was best, I am sure our growth and happiness would have stopped. My first husband Greg had doubts just like Paul. Then, my ego took hold and I willfully forced the situation, because I believed I was so right. Through my ego, I was trying to control another. Even though Greg has free will and could have left at any time, I believe my energy influenced him to marry me when he really didn't want to.

Greg and I are good friends, but in many painful ways we were not right for each other. I believe our conflicts kept arising so we could come to terms with what we needed to learn. My ego wanted my life to be a certain way, but if I had come more from a deeper spiritual awareness of life at that time, I believe we would have been separated sooner because we would have passed through our lessons faster. Maybe we would never have married each other.

I learned more in my year with Paul than in any previous time in my life. I know I will consistently grow and feel happier. Some people will be in my life a short time, while others will be in it for my whole life. I am learning that the time frame of relationships is not as important as the lessons learned from them.

Forgiveness and Non-Judgment ❧

Two important keys that have helped me form better relationships with others and myself are forgiveness and non-judgment. They are very similar. Forgiveness is an attitude that is important to cultivate when we feel that we have been wronged. Being non-judgmental is an ongoing process. When you are non-judgmental and forgiving, you attain a higher consciousness.

Most people feel forgiveness means pardoning another person for an error or indiscretion. That view comes from the small ego. It implies you are above someone else, that you are the judge.

True forgiveness means you reach a point in consciousness that you realize no one is to blame for anything; no one is wrong. Whatever happens in a relationship is perfect for what you need as Soul to grow. So in the deeper understanding of life, there is no one to forgive; whatever happens in your life is perfect.

Forgiveness really means that eventually, if you are linked with your higher self and Spirit, you will consciously realize whatever transpired was perfect for your growth. You then can release all attachments to how you wanted a situation to turn out and you release all negative energy you have regarding that event or person. Then true impartial love can flow through you and from you.

Processing Your Emotions 🙠

That doesn't mean you won't have feelings when things happen to you or that you can't defend your boundaries if necessary. I definitely had strong feelings about Paul that I needed to process when we broke up. If I had kept thinking that Paul wronged me, my life's energy would have created negativity and affected my whole life negatively. I still went through feelings of anger and sadness to process my loss, but I came to an understanding there was no one to blame and what happened was perfect. In this understanding, I did not deny my emotions. I processed them through the stages of loss to facilitate my growth. To process any loss in your life, you have to feel or experience denial, anger, and sadness, and then you come to resolution about the situation. When I use the word "process" regarding your emotions, I mean you are allowing your emotions healthy avenues of expression. These avenues help you transform your emotional energy so that you can clearly be in the present moment. You bring them up to your consciousness to clear. When you repress your emotions or you express them with no resolution as to the cause of why you feel the way you do, you stop your growth. For example, if I had stayed angry at Paul or let myself stay sad, I could never had gotten on with my life. My emotional self would still have been in the relationship. So to go forward in my life, I had to allow myself to feel all the emotional stages necessary to process my grief over ending our relationship.

Overcoming Judgments and Facilitating Forgiveness ❧

When you live with an attitude of forgiveness and non-judgment, it is easier to heal your emotional self, because you are beginning to live your life from a higher awareness. The more judgments you remove from your thinking, the better your relationships will become with everyone, including yourself. When you release judgments, you open your heart to love.

Being non-judgmental takes a more pervasive part in your life. It affects every relationship you have, including the one with yourself. When you judge yourself or others on how they live, you are coming from your ego. You are saying your way of living is right or your way of being is the only way. Judgments with your attitude and energy create blocks in relationships. If you are judging, you think your way is the only way of doing, being, or having. Judging can also be attitudes or thoughts that you hold about a person for something he or she is, did, or has.

Being a human being means you will have opinions. Know that you are entitled to your opinions, but also know that preferences and opinions are different than judgments. I may like the color blue, but I try not to tell others or hold the attitude that blue is the only "right" color.

The goal is to clear away obstructions in your thinking or actions that keep love and Spirit from flowing through you for yourself and others. Judgments are energy blocks that keep you from growing and loving.

I am going to leave you with a contemplation to increase your love for others and help you overcome judgments and facilitate forgiveness, thus improving your relationships.

Overcoming Judgments

Get in a comfortable sitting position. Close your eyes and gently focus your energy on the area between your eyes. Chant the word "HU" this time, because it opens your heart to love. Chant "HU" for 10 to 20 minutes, and bring up as much of a feeling of love as you can. If you have to remember a time when you felt love to bring up a love feeling, do that. Then visualize yourself surrounded with a pink light. The pink color here represents love. In this visualization, picture people who have relationships with you. Visualize either angels (or some highly-evolved, thoroughly-loving beings) milling or floating about you and the people in the relationship(s) that you want to heal. See the other people surrounded by the pink light. You and the other people are protected by the spiritual beings. Then imagine the people peeling off the physical body, which represents the physical ego or limitations of the human consciousness. Next see them as a body of brilliant light. (If you ever saw the movie *Cocoon* where the aliens peeled off their bodies and their real bodies were light, that's what I want you to imagine.)

Next surround the other people with that pink light. Think about any negative energy or feelings you have about the other people. See yourself giving it to the spiritual beings and see them taking your negative stuff away. (Let me remind you again that you should never do this or any other visualization to change or influence another person. Contemplations and visualizations are for your growth and healing regarding any situation.) ❧

You may have to do this contemplation (or one of your own) many times. Your aim is to get to a place of peace within yourself about a particular person or relationship. You can even do this for just yourself to really get the feel that your true self is Soul and not this body or ego. The more actions you take to relate to yourself and others from the belief and viewpoint of your spiritual self, the more this life makes sense and the more complete you will feel.

EXERCISE

Forgiveness

Another way to do this contemplation is to once again chant "HU" for 10 to 20 minutes. Then see the person you have problems with. Repeat to yourself after you have chanted HU, "I forgive you for anything that you may have done to me in the past, present, or future. I also forgive myself for anything I may have done to you in the past, present, or future." This is extremely powerful! These statements, when done sincerely, can help you eliminate negative energy between yourself and the other person.

Relating is an ongoing process. Try to remember to relate in a vibrant and ever-opening way. As you take actions to relate to life, yourself, and others in this fashion, a new dimension will start to emerge. You will begin to feel a new aliveness and depth with all the people in your life, including yourself! ✴

Epilog

Remember the saying, "If you love something, set it free, and if it was meant to be, it will come back to you"? It is true! Paul and I broke up, but he came back, and we are married!

Paul and I wanted to be free of co-dependency in marriage, and our year-long separation helped us confront ourselves in exactly the way we needed to heal this issue. We also both wanted Spiritually-oriented partners. During the time we were separated, I truly thought that it was over for good, but I never lost sight of uniting with Spirit for my highest purpose. Both Paul and I concentrated on personal development during the time we were separated and even dated other people.

About one week after I finished the first draft of this book, Paul came to Atlanta to finish some business regarding our house. We found we still felt a deep connection and love for each other. We had many long conversations, and we both found we had grown stronger while we were apart. We still wanted the same things out of life. There were no doubts this time. Once again he asked me to marry him, and this time all was in order!

Our relationship and our eventual marriage is a perfect example of how, sometimes, we seem to encounter roadblocks when, in truth, we have found the fastest road to our destination. Paul and I learned valuable lessons in trusting Spirit, getting our needs met, and staying detached about what we thought is the "correct" outcome.

Be true to yourself and shoot for the highest you can possibly be. All that is good for your life will manifest!

Love

Love is the power
that heals,
uplifts,
brings joy and light
into your life.

Love is the power
that creates
All,
that is beautiful, abundant
and good.

Love is the power,
when nurtured,
it
changes the course
of your life.

Love is the power
as you accept it
from Spirit,
you can accomplish
ANYTHING! ❧

Chapter 6

Love

Love is constantly on people's minds. The human race has a deep fascination with love. It's depicted constantly through songs, books, and movies. Love is the most precious and beautiful experience you can have! Love is also the most mysterious and confusing of your emotions. With this chapter I'll explain what love is, clarify how you can attain more of it in your life, and, eventually, how to evolve your love to the highest form and express it in the purest way.

What Is Love? 🙠

In your lifetime you will experience many kinds of love. There is the love that parents have for their children, love for one's lover or mate, the love that you have for friends, and so on. But what is love? People say they are experiencing love or that they are in love. But what is this emotion we all call "love"?

This question takes me to an experience I had at a spiritual seminar that was designed to help the individual grow toward God in one's own unique way. I was attending this seminar with all my best friends and my sister Joan. I knew when I got back home I was going to start writing this chapter, so my mind was focused on love. We had been at this seminar for three days, and on the last day we all decided to have brunch together before we were to go home.

During brunch, the question, "What is love?" popped into my mind. So I asked that question of everyone at the

131

table because I felt I needed a little feedback. I was feeling a little uneasy about this chapter, because understanding love is so important and I wanted to convey this understanding as clearly as possible.

Now my friends love, I mean adore, talking about the different aspects of life and growth. We are all passionate about this kind of communication. So now you have all these people who have been spirituality submerged for three days, who adore talking about life as much as they need to breathe, and when I asked them about love they ignored my question. This was out of character for everyone there; consequently their lack of response had a powerful impact on me.

I have been working with Spirit long enough to feel that their lack of response was not out of rudeness or insensitivity. I felt it was Spirit's way of teaching me I already had the answer. The waking dream that rang true for me was that each individual has the inner awareness of what love truly is. We ALL have all the answers inside ourselves as Soul.

I am learning to always look to Spirit to guide me in my life. I believe the writing of this book has been guided by Spirit and that incident during our brunch was a lesson for me about trust, to trust myself and Spirit. So as it happened, no matter how much I prodded them, I couldn't get anyone to answer my question. I also think love is impossible to put into words. A true and deep understanding of love is a knowing and an experience that comes from your heart and Soul.

Now this makes my job even harder. I am writing a chapter on something that can't be known with words! Instead of giving a definition of love, I'm going to describe some basic characteristics of love and the different kinds of love you can experience.

Loving Yourself ❧

The first avenue of expressing love is loving yourself. True self-love is giving and opening your heart to Spirit or God and letting the wonderful light energy of the positive flow through your being. It is loving your flaws and imperfections through all your life lessons. When you love and accept yourself fully, every aspect of your life flourishes. I just can't emphasize self-love enough!

If your heart is closed to yourself, how can it be open for others? Your heart is the gateway of and to God and Spirit. Self-love is the food and the seed of all other love and positive things in your life. Many people think self-love is negative selfishness. I definitely disagree. When you open your heart to loving yourself, you are opening the way to a deeper connection to God, who is love ITSELF, and ultimately to a deep love and positive energy for all of life. How can opening your heart to God and Spirit be bad? How can raising your vibrations be anything but good?

Too many people try to attain self-love by relating to others in a way that doesn't appear negative, but really is. Let's take the example of a person from a dysfunctional background who has not yet healed inner emotional traumas. This person might compensate for a lack of self-love by always giving to others. Giving to others is noble. I am not discounting the act of giving. But the *true* reason this person may be giving is because *unconsciously* he or she feels unloved. In this example, by giving to others, the person is trying to get the love in life that he or she has not received. The person is feeding a deep need within him—or herself.

Some people unconsciously feel that if they give enough, then they are worthwhile, and they will receive love. When, in fact, only when you love yourself fully first can you freely give to others.

Love As Energy ❧

This is a subtle distinction and one that needs to be addressed. To understand this distinction better, let's go back to the teaching that everything is energy.

If you are energy, everything about you vibrates or moves, because the intrinsic nature of energy is movement. If in your own life you are vibrating from lack (in this case the lack love), then when your energy intermingles with others, it will be vibrating from a state of lack. If you are in this state while you are in a romance, a friendship, or family structure, you really want something from these other people. You want their love energy to fill an emptiness within yourself. So in a very true sense, you are taking something from them. You are not giving or being a truly open vehicle for Spirit, as you might believe.

Love is a condition of positive, fulfilled consciousness. Since love is energy, it needs to flow, just like a stream or river needs to flow to be pure. When you are in the *highest* state of loving, you are an open vehicle for the light and sound of Spirit to flow through you **without** ego attachments. Taking someone else's energy is not a pure form of love. If you have complete self-love, you give to others with **no expectations** of wanting anything from them, and at the same time, you protect your own boundaries and fulfill your own needs. You are able to do this because you have more than enough love flowing through your life already. You have to realize your own love in your life before you can share it successfully with anyone else. You cannot give out something you don't already possess!

Opening Your Heart ❧

I have found it is very hard for people to open their hearts to deep self-love or a complete opening of the heart to God and Spirit. This is enlightenment. True self-love is

Divine love. It is limitless, just as God is limitless. Because our truest natures are Spirit, when we close our hearts off to ourselves, we close our hearts off to Spirit and God.

There may be people who can open their hearts to others and in the process have their own hearts open to themselves. But I find more individuals running into problems because of a lack of self-love, rather than the other way around.

Self-love is not sitting around and adoring yourself. (That is not love; that is negative energy from the ego.) Someone experiencing deep self-love has the energy and the desire to serve Spirit through individual awakening and whatever else Spirit wants one to do for others. Self-love is an ongoing, evolving expansion that spills over to everyone in your life, without losing yourself in the process. When you are always full and in touch with the source of love, you have an endless supply of love for all of life!

Why Self-Love Is Important ❧

This kind of self-love opens your heart to God and balances you in all of your bodies. You allow yourself to rest when you need to rest, and you have fun when you need to have fun. Self-love is not abusing yourself with guilt when you are giving yourself what you need. Self-love expresses itself in positive appreciation for your own uniqueness and feeling your worth as Soul. Self-love and self-worth are closely tied together. It's hard to feel worthy if you don't love yourself.

In my own life, I find that the more I love and respect myself, the more I am truly able to give love from my heart to others, without strings attached. When I felt unworthy, I had no energy or love to give others. My relationships with men were co-dependent and I tried to get my worth and internal self-love from their approval. My taking responsibility for others and negating myself for a man's love was my way of trying to get love and worth for myself. If I already had love internally, I wouldn't have put up with the abuse I attracted. I would have been myself no matter what.

The more love I allow myself while connecting with Spirit, the deeper and more satisfying my relationships are with all people. When the core of my being is connected to Spirit, I have love energy to give without having to draw other people's energy back into myself. When I have this connection to Spirit and love within myself, I feel the balance between my inflow from myself and Spirit and my outflow to others. You will find yourself growing faster because of this balanced love flow.

EXERCISE

Loving Yourself More Fully

To love yourself fully, you have to know what parts of yourself are shut off from love. This exercise will help you pinpoint parts of yourself that need your love and care.

Take a piece of paper and draw a line down the middle. On the left side of the paper, list all parts of yourself you dislike, hate, or ignore. (These parts can be body parts, emotional ways of dealing with life, or aspects of your intelligence. Other parts of yourself are your male and female sides, adult self, or child self. For example, if you have a hard time asserting yourself or making decisions, this could be an indication of not loving your male self. This can be true whether you are a man or a woman, for we all have male and female parts of ourselves. If you have a hard time having fun or being in the now, your little child may need some love. And so on.) Really take some time with this and get to know yourself thoroughly and honestly. The benefactor will be you.

On the right side, list all the aspects of yourself that you like and consciously know you love. Now schedule some uninterrupted time for yourself, at least 20 minutes. Put some soothing music on. (Sound or music impacts imagery. Extensive research in this field has found sound or music can double the absorption of imagery in the unconscious mind. So whenever you do imagery work, try to have soothing music in the background.)

Imagine a very safe place. (It can be a room or a nature setting.) Feel totally safe and secure and ready for growth. Visualize yourself meeting all the parts you listed on the left side of your paper. One by one, love, honor, and thank them for all they have done for you.

Validate their existence. The more you validate them, the easier it will be to transform them to a new, more satisfying role.

Work with all the left side parts until you have complete love and appreciation for their existence. This may take more than one session. Be aware of any beliefs or feelings which emerge. If they are invalidating in any way, deal with them with the same method. Treat any negative beliefs that arise as separate parts of yourself that need to be validated and transformed. After you have reached this point, forgive yourself for negating any part of yourself.

Next, introduce the right side parts to the left. Let them love each other and feel needed. If you want to change or strengthen certain parts, now is the time to do it. For example, if you are overweight and haven't loved your thighs, communicate to your thighs that you have appreciated their support of your body and life. Now give them a new and more important job. They can be thinner and still support you. Tell them you will love them ALWAYS!

If you are a woman and have been attracting negative relationships, you may not be loving the male part of yourself. Talk to that part and reassure it that you will always love it. Introduce it to your female part and reassure this part that as your male part gets healthier, so will she. Tell them they are both important to you. Keep doing this until all your parts feel loved, useful, and worthy. 🕊

Doing this exercise can help you unblock areas of yourself that need healing and love. You may uncover beliefs that were hindering your growth. By unblocking yourself, you open yourself for healthier relationships with others. The more we love ourselves, the more love we allow into our lives from others.

Understanding Love 🕊

When you block loving yourself or receiving love from others, the flow of love is out of balance, and someone, either you or another, becomes a victim. This is especially true with romantic love, because your boundaries are so hard to keep in place. You cannot continue to stay balanced and grow healthily if you give romantic or emotional love to someone who does not return your love. Love, like any energy, needs to continually move and flow. So if another person does not accept your love, love is blocked from flowing.

Romantic Love ❧

Most of us have experienced romantic love. It starts when you meet someone and all the boundaries between the two of you come down. In the first stages, the other person seems perfect in most every way. There is a balanced flow of energy; each person is giving and receiving love energy on the personal, emotional, intellectual, and in some cases, even the spiritual level. Interpersonal, individual, emotional, mental, and spiritual growth can be best achieved when both people are open (giving and receiving) on all levels.

Ultimately I feel the truest and highest reason two people are in a romantic relationship is to grow Spiritually. When we have a romantic relationship with someone, especially in marriage, many doors are open for learning, healing, and growing. Love opens the way for growth!

When Love Is Blocked ❧

But if that strong love energy becomes blocked at either end, it can cause the people in the relationship to suffer. This blockage occurs when either party no longer wants to communicate or grow with the same depth or speed as the other. Personal love—romantic love—needs an opening for energy to be received **and** given. If blockages occur, the best way to salvage the relationship is for the relationship to be restructured to one of impersonal (Divine) love. The person in the relationship wanting more love should stop giving that intense romantic love, because the other person is not ready to exchange their love or accept love in the romantic, personal way.

Now, personally, I try never to tell another what to do. With this example, I am expressing actions one can take to go forward. No one knows what experiences another may need to grow toward God. So some people may need this experience to understand how this flow of love works or for other lessons as Soul. But if you are experiencing this, contemplate the best course of action for you.

Love Needs Actions to Grow ❧

Love, whether it is personal or Divine, requires continual action to grow. Love is not just a nice "warm fuzzy" or a place where you arrive and languish. You need to continually give to yourself what you need. When you are in a healthy relationship with another, it may have its ups and downs. Each party needs to act to keep the love flowing. When each individual is committed to the health, growth, and love of themselves and the other, only good can occur.

The time frame for realizing a relationship has changed is different for all relationships. Once you realize there is no hope of equal exchange the pattern of love needs to change. If you continue to give emotional, romantic love to someone who cannot reciprocate, you are placing yourself as a victim. You are using your power or energy passively. This becomes a one-way street. You are creating negative actions when you consistently send energy or personal love to someone who cannot receive it.

Your life will reflect this in many ways. Maybe constant arguments or disharmony of some sort will manifest in your relationship. Maybe, if you are the one sending out the unwanted love, you will start to feel powerless and lose energy or something will feel off kilter in your life or as a couple.

Loving from Personal Power ❧

A relationship or love exchange is coming from a positive place when both parties are at cause in their life, coming from personal power. (When I use the word "power" here or anywhere in this book, I am referring to a state of consciousness of connecting with Spirit in creating your life. This means you are at cause in your life and consciously taking actions to create your life with the most value.) The relationship will then grow in a positive way with harmonious effects on both your lives. Look to the workings of your daily life to know how love is flowing in your life.

You become powerless when you are wanting and waiting for another person's love, and it is not forthcoming. You are at the mercy of their actions and have relinquished your power of creating. This is what causes suffering in romantic relationships. It can happen in other personal relationships as well. This does not make anyone wrong. It could be an indication of tremendous growth for all concerned. Everyone needs different experiences to grow, and many times when you are growing the most, your relationships can change in a very quick way. You may be experiencing lessons with someone in a year or two that otherwise would take a lifetime.

Learning from Love ❧

Let me give you an example. In the beginning, when Paul and I exchanged personal love, our energy and our commitment to ourselves as individuals and as a couple had an even flow to it. During our first few months together, we were both receivers and givers of love. When Paul moved to Atlanta (and maybe even before that time), there was a subtle shift in his energy and attention to the relationship as a whole. I felt the change immediately, but

I denied it because I didn't want it to happen. At first I felt that it was from his moving from his own country to a new city and country. Around this same time, he had found out his father was ill. I felt all these things were affecting him, but it was none of those things. He was withdrawing his romantic love from our relationship, as I found out later, for the growth of his self as Soul.

In our physical realm, there is a difference in the kinds of love one gives. When individuals are not clear about the differences, personal boundaries, and expectations, it causes problems. Paul needed time outside a committed relationship to grow. Even though he still loved me, he was not able to commit, to me or to our relationship, the love I wanted for a long-term relationship and marriage.

This period in our lives was very confusing for both of us. We loved each other, yet we each had to take actions that were the best for our individual growth. So during the time of Paul's sorting out what was best for his growth as Soul, I felt the withdrawal of his energy from me and from us as a couple. This change in him shifted how we could relate.

At first I tried to give more romantic love, and at the same time give him space. The more I gave romantic love to him when he was not capable of receiving it or reciprocating, the more I felt alone and rejected. And later, I learned the more I gave, the more he felt smothered. I was operating from effect, the powerless stance of being a victim. This always is negative. ("Negative" here does not mean a shaming way, but a way that is not coming from your personal power of a creator.) And because I was operating from the negative, my energy was being drained in every way. When you make negative actions, it can drain your energy. This drain affected my work, my health, and my creativity. No one was creating or causing this drain but me.

The Importance of Balanced Love Flow ⤇

At that time there was not a balanced flow of energy between us. (I know all relationships go through their ups and downs. This is normal and a response to the growth periods of the two individuals. This is not what I am talking about here.) A separation of energies such as Paul and I had is a major breakdown of two people relating as a couple. As time passed, I had to face the reality that Paul needed to go his own way. It truly was the best thing in the long run, but it felt like the end of our relationship.

I had to realize there was no longer an exchange of the kind of deep and romantic love that was necessary for our relationship to work out. Paul needed to shut off accepting that kind of love from me, and I suffered greatly. His closing his heart to me in this way was not something I wanted to live with. I thought it might take years for him to want to work as a couple. We both understood that to keep giving out love energy that can't be reciprocated is unhealthy for both parties.

If I had continued to give him romantic love when he could not reciprocate, I would have been a victim. (Remember victims are powerless in their lives because they do not claim their spiritual power to create the lives they want.) I had to make a shift from loving Paul romantically to one of an impersonal love from my spiritual nature. I now had to give him Divine love only, if I wanted to be happy and healthy, for I wanted always to love him. But on this plane and for that time, the only love we were able to share healthily was Divine spiritual love.

When I started to switch my romantic love energy to one coming from just one Soul loving another Soul, I started reclaiming my power. Relinquishing the need or the attachment of that romantic connection was the key to regaining my health and power. You can only grow when you are in the consciousness of being at cause (a creator) and not at effect (a victim). Remember, actions made from personal power create value for your growth and self-worth. When I started to be at cause and reclaim my power over my own life, my suffering lessened.

That time in our lives was extremely powerful for us. Both of us really implemented self-love. This helped us heal inner issues about childhood and created a strong foundation for our marriage. The more you allow self-love to grow, even in romantic relationships, the more positive the outcome will be.

Flow of Love 🍃

I bring up the concept of flow because I feel most people do not realize how important keeping an open flow can be. So many people suffer because they are unaware of how energy affects their lives. If you are constantly giving personal energy to people with an attitude of attachment to its outcome or to people who are incapable of receiving this energy, you will suffer.

Everything you do, feelings included, is affected on this plane of existence by Cause and Effect. Every action has a reaction. This is an example of energy that is blocked from flowing. If you keep putting water into a container and the water has no way to move or be emptied, then the water will spill out and probably cause a mess. The same holds true when you give your personal energy to others who are incapable or not willing to receive it, only you find the mess is in your own life. Remember, energy needs to keep moving.

Problems of Attachment ❧

You may not be aware of problems in your life caused by your attachment or persistent flow of energy to another person. This imbalance of the flow of your energy is really a disregard for another person's boundaries. You are forcing part of yourself (your energy or love) into someone's space without their permission. That is why it is negative. You must have the permission or willingness of the other person to receive your love or energy to have a positive relationship and effect in your life. Their permission comes very rarely with their words. You have to look and observe their actions and reactions to your giving. Remember, actions always speak louder than words.

Understanding Personal Love ❧

So many of us are taught to give personal love strongly to just anyone or to people we feel are needy. We are also taught to give our personal love whether the other person abuses it or not. I am in total agreement with giving impersonal or Divine love to all. When you give Divine love, you are expressing your love not from your human consciousness or the wants of your ego, but from yourself as Soul. When you express love in this way, the love energy aligns with Spirit and God. It is given freely without attachments. Romantic love and other kinds of personal love come from parts of our lower self—like the emotional body or mind—and these forms of love carry with them attachments regarding an outcome.

Since you are energy, you give YOUR ENERGY when you give personal love to others. When others can't accept it or when they abuse your gift, the flow is stopped and you could suffer because of this. It is similar to trying to fill up a glass with water when it has a lid on it. The water will go everywhere except in the glass. Divine love is like sunshine on the glass of water. Even when the lid is on the glass, the sunlight can get through. The sunlight is not affected by the water or the glass having a lid on it. The sun represents the limitless source, power, and detachment of Divine love.

Divine Love ❧

When I talk about Divine love, I mean giving love from a place in Soul which is in union with Spirit and God. It is a place where personal energy is not going to be abused or used. Divine love is a gift from God through one person to another. It is impersonal and unattached. The more personal or romantic the love becomes, the more careful you have to be not to overstep people's boundaries or become co-dependent.

Techniques of Opening Up to Love ❧

How do you go about creating a consciousness or a state of being that has more love? One of the first steps in creating anything, including love, is to know you can create it. Knowing you have the power to create is fundamental. Without this knowing, you are left without hope and direction in your life.

If the direction in your life is to achieve more love in your outer world, you have to start with changing your inner self or inner world. Change always follows the course of inner to outer. When you change your inner self, your outer environment changes. This is why self-love has to come first, so you can manifest more love in your outer worlds.

To make a comprehensive change in your life, it is better to use every level—Soul, the mind (conscious and unconscious), the emotions, and the physical body—to achieve that change. When you use these parts in unison to achieve change, you manifest your desires faster.

Importance of Sincerity ❧

One of the most important aspects of creating more love in your life is sincerity. This is the state of consciousness that Christ talked about when he spoke of being like a little child. Sincerity goes right to your depths, right to Soul, right through to Spirit. It is the big open eyes of a child, open to see everything. It is trust and letting down the ego barriers of the small self and openly stating that what you want in your life is the deep love of Spirit. Sincerity means that you are not too grown up, too smart, or too knowledgeable to want this state of consciousness. It's a wanting and a hunger from your heart for the flow of Divine love to enter your being.

Now I am going to take you through different exercises to help you open the different parts of yourself, so that you can accept more love into your life on every level. At any time when you use these exercises, follow your intuition. Maybe for one day or for a few weeks, you will be using one exercise. Then it may become clear to you to stop using that particular exercise and use another. Trust your instincts.

For instance, maybe you've realized that the flow of love is stopped because of a belief you've been holding about your self-worth. So maybe the exercises dealing with the mind might be appropriate. Or maybe you are frozen on an emotional level, with fears that you can't pinpoint. Then the best exercises to work with would be ones that deal with your emotional body. Allow yourself to know what you need to do to achieve change, so you can acquire this love in your life. Remember, the love you seek is already in your life as Soul. It is just your blocks that keep you from experiencing love fully in the present moment.

How to Expand Love

Any spiritual exercise in this book will help you open up to yourself as Soul and to Spirit. Use any exercises alone or in combination with others. One exercise that you can do is to chant a high vibratory word, with your eyes closed, sitting in a comfortable position. Focus on the area between your eyes. Do this for about 10 to 15 minutes each day for a month. (Some high vibratory words again are "HU," "God," "Wah Z," or "Love.")

Consistency is very important. Be lovingly committed to your time of contemplation. Your 10 to 15 minutes a day in contemplation is the very fuel you need to raise your vibrations and quality of life. Pick a time when you won't be interrupted. This time for yourself could be in the morning, in the middle of the day, or right before you go to bed, but do give yourself this time.

After you have chanted your word, visualize yourself as a body of shimmering light, as you think Soul would look. Imagine yourself in a beautiful place filled with light. It could be a beautiful structure made up of light or a nature setting, but see it beautiful, peaceful, and secure. Imagine, see, and feel the area where your heart is in your body, being filled with this light and warmth. Some of the colors you could see in your heart area are pink, gold, or a bright white.

See your heart area expanding and radiating outward with light. Listen for sounds. If you hear any, allow them to fill your being. Keep imagining your heart expanding and allow yourself to feel totally secure. Then bring the picture of yourself filled with light down to a setting in your daily life. Hold on to the feeling of security and the loving energy, because that light is the love you are seeking. When you feel you have completed this exercise, finish with a inner appreciation that love is a part of you and your life right now. This action of appreciation brings home that everything is already here for you. You just have to be in an aware state of consciousness to accept it. ❧

Affirmations

Something else you can do are affirmations. (All these exercises will affect many parts of you simultaneously.) These affirmations must be written in the present tense and done with feeling. Writing in longhand reaches the unconscious mind and facilitates acceptance at the mental level. Some affirmations you can do are: "I am filled with the light and sound of God." "More and more each day I am accepting love from Spirit." "More and more each day I am feeling

God's love." "I am letting the love of God and Spirit flow through me." "I am living as love more and more each day." "I am worthy of God's love, now."

You also can make up your own affirmations. Trust your intuition and create affirmations accordingly. Writing them out before you go to bed is an extremely powerful way of reaching the unconscious mind. ✍

Something you can do for your physical self that will open yourself up to love is by acting as if you are love. Start using your body in loving ways. Remember, there is no separation between your body, mind, and emotions. Actions on any level affect all parts of yourself.

EXERCISE

Acting As Love

When people are of a loving nature, they find it easy to smile. They have a presence of relaxed security and radiate warmth and kindness. So smile more! Smiling and laughter change the chemistry in the body. People feel more open and receptive around individuals who smile.

The smiling I am talking about is not the shallow, pasted-on smile of insincerity. For this exercise you need to practice smiling from your heart. When you smile from the depths of your heart, your face follows. Smile this way to yourself when you are in front of a mirror and practice sending yourself love. When you see your eyes in your mirror, really see your Spirit and your Soul. Allow yourself to smile from your heart. Give yourself the love that comes from Spirit. If you feel uncomfortable about giving yourself love and joy, then the love that you give others will be limited, because you can only give out to others what you possess or are able to receive.

When you are in love with someone, it is easy to do nice things for that person. You are showing and expressing love on the physical level by your actions. How often do you show yourself love by your actions? Examine your train of thought. How positive and loving are your thoughts to yourself? How much time do you give yourself to support yourself in your growth? Most of us walk around mentally beating ourselves up and never doing nice things for ourselves or appreciating our own beingness. ॐ

Allow love to flow through YOU as well as to others. When you allow it to flow through you and outward in a detached way to others, you increase the amount of love you are capable of experiencing. It is similar to exercising your body; the more you move your body, the better and healthier your body gets. The more you let your body atrophy, the less it is capable of doing. The more actions you make with accepting love within yourself and allowing it to flow outward, the more love will grow in your own heart.

The very action of asking for more love will lead you to manifest this love. Trust, and take action consistently. Open your heart and let it be filled with the love that you seek. Love is nowhere else but inside your very being!

Balance

It drives you crazy
going from this to that
up and then down
inside and then out.
Peddling as fast as you can,
to find out that you
are already there
or didn't need to go.

Total juggling act.
At times all is in
perfect harmony and peace,
but once again you are on your way.
Growth ever–calling your name
having to rearrange once again
what is up, what is down
and what have you found . . .
That balance is not a stagnant state,
nothing ever to be disturbed,
but a consistent rearrangement
of the ever-growing you. ॐ

Chapter 7

Balance

Most people don't know what balance is and how important it is in life. Without balance you cannot be all you can be, because some part of you will be ineffective or overcompensating for the rest of you. Let me explain how balance relates to every aspect of your life.

The Parts of Us ❧

Being human means you are composed of many bodies, integral yet separate. We can readily understand we have a physical body, so let's take this understanding to a new level. Next, think of the mind, emotions, and Soul as separate bodies, or parts, of us. All these parts have different needs. These parts comprise the total person.

It is much easier to understand what you need as a person and how to get your needs met when you have a better comprehension of the functions and needs of each separate part. Each person (including you) is comprised of Soul, a physical body, the mind (which includes the conscious and unconscious), and the emotional self.

The spiritual, emotional, and mental parts of you are not truly separate from your whole being or your physical self, though they do need separate and direct care. All these separate parts are linked together through Soul. When you act from a spiritual understanding that your truest, indestructible self is Soul, you can function more fully in this physical dimension.

Keeping the whole of yourself in balance is a tremen-

155

dous vehicle for self-growth and self-mastery. Balance is necessary for self-mastery, because when you are in balance, you are more open to Spirit flowing through you. If one or more of your bodies is out of balance, it keeps you from being conscious and aware of your higher self. It is important to consider all parts of you for the completion of your highest development.

Balance is another name for harmony. Harmony is important, because without it, you are fighting within yourself. If you are out of balance, you cannot grow as you could when all parts of you are unified and nurtured. It is like the saying, "A house divided against itself cannot stand." When you know the requirements of each part, you can furnish exactly what each needs to heal and grow while staying unified.

You are the most effective and you can achieve the most in your life when all parts of you are happy and healthy. If you decide not to take care of yourself as a whole, you live with the consequences of being less than you could be. You don't have to do anything. You have free will, but you will always receive the consequences of your choices in life. And this holds true for how you treat all the different parts of yourself as well.

The Physical Body ❧

The first part of you is the most obvious part, your physical body. Even though it is the part most people can relate to easily, it is still woefully neglected. Most of us were brought up with the belief there is always a doctor or pill that can fix what ails you. This breeds a lack of responsibility toward our bodies and how we treat them.

So what is a balanced body, and what can you do to facilitate health and harmony in your body? Many people have a hard time accomplishing the necessary, daily things to maintain health and keep their bodies balanced and running smoothly. So how can you learn what to do for your health without your becoming a doctor or studying nutrition for years?

Let me state right here, I'm not a physician or nutritionist. My suggestions are just that, suggestions. Ultimately, each individual has to find out what is correct for his or her personal health and well-being. What I am offering are suggestions from my own experiences—what has worked for me—and suggestions from nutritionists and health professionals. You can use this information in your life if it seems correct to you. What is most important is for you to take an active role in your health.

Being Aware of What You Need ❧

My own awareness of health started when I observed my mother. She was sick my whole life. Her sickness made me very aware that without health, you really can't give to anyone fully or be all you want to be in your life. When I left home, I was a mess emotionally and I was abusing my body with cigarettes, drugs, and alcohol, and I was a full-blown bulimic. I was not doing much to help my body in a positive way. Needless to say, this was not a balanced lifestyle! Before I left home, I didn't realize how much control I could have regarding my health.

My older brother Marty planted the seeds of nutrition and self–responsibility of how I now treat my body. Marty was into vitamins and pure water and exercise way before it was the rage. At that time we all thought he was a little strange to take all those vitamins and to spend time exercising. But now I do a lot of what he was doing then.

At 21, I felt I was an old 40. I was constantly without energy and always getting sick, especially with bronchitis. So I started to pursue health, energy, and vitality. As I learned about Cause and Effect and started to incorporate it into my daily life, I realized that how I treated my body DID make a difference. One of the first things I did was to quit smoking. Quitting smoking wasn't easy, but it was important for my health, and it started me on the road to a healthier way of life.

In trying to find a healthier and more balanced physical self, I learned our bodies do need all the basics we were taught. We all need to drink plenty of clean water each day. We need quiet time, like contemplation. We need to eat more raw fruits and vegetables than cooked food. The body needs to be exercised regularly and exposed to fresh air and sunlight. This is not startling news to anyone. As you may already have concluded, the truths of life are very simple, but following these truths consistently can be difficult.

Everybody's body chemistry is different, and your requirements may be different than other people's in order for you to maintain balanced health. This is because each individual is always changing in every regard. You will know if a food or an exercise is right for you because with it you will start to feel clearer, happier, or more energized. It is this simple. The key to having a healthier body is observing the simple cause-and-effect relationships in your life. This will give you many answers to your life problems, even down to the basics of what kinds of food and exercise are right for you.

I listen to my body and observe how it feels at different times. I pay attention to what happens to it with the types of food I eat, how it feels after different kinds of exercise, and when it needs rest. I have learned that lots of sugar or junk foods detract from my energy, and I emotionally feel down when I eat too much of these foods. Exercise, for me, is vital for staying energized and mentally happy. Personally, I need lots of sunlight and lots and lots of water or I just feel lousy. I am aware that if I work too much indoors, sitting with clients or writing, my body starts to ache.

Because I have taken responsibility for my vitality and health for years, I look younger now than I did five years ago, and I have more energy and mental clarity than ever. I hardly ever get sick!

As I progress in my search for health and a balanced body, there are some things I no longer do that I did before, and some things I'll keep doing. Personal health is the responsibility of each individual. What might be marvelous for me might not be great for you. What might be good for you now may not be right for you in the future. Life is change. Stay in the present to find out what is best for your life.

Let me give you an example. When I first started to exercise, a half-mile jog almost killed me! Now I run three miles and enjoy it. Maybe yoga or walking is more suited for your body and life-style. You have to be the judge about any exercise or diet and how it affects your life and well-being.

I have also tried many different ways of eating, from macrobiotic to complete vegetarianism to fasting. I have experimented with just about every way of eating. I have concluded that no matter how balanced the diet might be, if I don't like it or it doesn't fit my life-style, then I won't consistently use it. Recently, I needed to find an easier way to eat healthily that I would do consistently. I was in a quandary as to how to get more vegetables into my diet.

When the answers are not obvious, I go within and ask Spirit to guide me, because Spirit knows all. Spirit answered me through my great friend Beth. I hate to cook day after day and I don't enjoy salads, so I find it hard to consistently get vegetables in my diet. One day Beth told me about making fresh vegetable juice and drinking it every day. She said she had read that the body absorbs nutrients nine times more effectively from fresh juices than from eating the raw or cooked vegetables alone. This method has been perfect for me lately. You may find something better suited to you. Just give yourself the permission to know and hear the answers that are right for you. Maybe you will find an answer from a good friend or maybe when you read something, an answer will become obvious to you. When you have questions regarding your health or diet, know the answers are there. Be open to discovering them.

Not taking care of your body is a way of blocking self-love. When you are taking care of yourself, you send out loving energy, and that vibration will be felt by your friends and family. You are taking positive actions and creating good energy or karma when you take care of yourself.

Sickness ❧

When we get sick or cranky we are out of balance, and being out of balance limits our potential for a greater life and for Spirit to flow positively through our lives. I know when I don't feel well I am less likely to be kind or giving to anyone, because all my energy is being used inwardly to help me get better.

Listen to your body. If you feel tired, rest. Sickness can be caused by many things, but lots of times you get sick simply because your body is telling you it is tired. Or sickness can be a way your body reacts to food that is bad for you. Your body getting sick can be a message that there might be emotional issues to address that you have been avoiding.

Most people tell me they don't know what their bodies need. What I usually tell these people is to act as if you know what the body needs and the answers will come to you. This is what is meant by becoming more aware. Talk to your body. Ask Spirit to guide you to a person or a solution to help you know what you need to do next. Remember, you will always get the answers to your questions through Spirit if you ask and then consistently take actions.

If I can come from being abusive about my health to a place where I am guided and know what I need for my body's balance, so can you. I am not different than anyone else. The answers and help you will receive are contingent on how badly you want to change and how honestly you confront yourself, so act on those desires and answers.

The Emotional Body

The emotional self is hard for some people to deal with, because emotions aren't tangible and because most of us have been taught to suppress our feelings. Suppressing feelings is a main cause of emotional imbalance.

Emotional balance means an individual has healthy self-esteem and a sense of self-worth. Emotionally balanced people are not afraid to feel what they need to feel when they feel it. Most people live life from the neck up. They handle life on a strictly intellectual basis.

If you were abused in childhood or came from a dysfunctional home, you learned to stuff all those neglected inner child feelings away because it wasn't safe at that time to feel them. It might have been safer for you to handle your life from the intellect alone. Now, you might think if you intellectually understand something, then you don't need to feel the emotion(s) involved in order for you to heal. When we come from this perspective about life, we limit our healing and perhaps block it altogether. Remember, your mind and emotions are distinct, different parts of you as a person, so they need distinct and different methods of healing and nurturing. Problems arise when we neglect to give any of our parts the healing and nurturing they need.

Let me give you an example. I came from a dysfunctional childhood and my nurturing needs for my own inner child were not met. I suppressed hurt and anger over my childhood for years. Those feelings were not gone because I suppressed them, they were just hidden from my conscious mind. Hiding my feelings made me feel worse and limited my effectiveness as a person. Repressing my emotions affected me in concrete, negative ways.

Even as a child, I understood my mother was sick and she did the best she could for me, but this intellectual understanding didn't help me heal my emotional self. I thought if I understood the situation, I wouldn't feel angry or hurt because my mother couldn't nurture me the way I needed. I tried to bypass my emotional healing through my intellectual understanding. Because I denied my feelings, I subconsciously created different ways to act out my suppressed feelings of anger and low self-worth. I did this through drinking, drugs, and bulimia.

Many of my clients are amazed to learn they need to experience feelings in order to be truly balanced and in harmony. Most people are shocked to learn many problems in their lives are caused by suppressed emotions. They think they are functioning okay when they cut themselves off from any or all of their feelings. But how okay is okay? You can go through life repressing your feelings and survive. But I wanted to be more than a survivor. I wanted to experience all I could be. As I grew in awareness, I knew that for me to be my happiest, most creative self, I'd have to heal the emotional part of me. I tell my clients that to heal your feelings you have to **feel them**, not just "think" them healed. Feeling your feelings is your key to creating a happy, balanced emotional self.

Balancing your emotional part means not only feeling present issues, but also clearing any negative emotional issues from your childhood. If your past emotions have not been dealt with, you are still living and reacting from them. When you've completely healed the emotional issues from your past, you are then able to truly live in the moment. You cannot be in control and create what you want in the present moment if you are reacting from past emotional pain or negative limiting beliefs.

Let me explain. Most of us have learned that there is some nurturing missing in our upbringing. This lack of nurturing can create repressed feelings of anger and low self-esteem. Maybe you understand your childhood but have never dealt with the hurtful feelings associated with it. Consequently, you will carry around those feelings for your entire life. These emotional energy vibrations are always in your life but are hidden until you become conscious of them and let them be acknowledged and felt. Repressed or denied feelings may manifest as an eating disorder, as I had, or as a drug or alcohol problem. Or you may have trouble with relationships or accepting loving and nurturing people around you. You might even be driven to be an over-achiever. There can be a multitude of scenarios. The old, unprocessed feelings **always** affect the decisions and actions you make and the quality of your life right now.

For example, a client named Maggie came to me to help her with relationships. In seven years, she didn't accept more than two dates in a row from any one man, because she always found something she didn't like about him. Maggie is not unattractive or disagreeable in her personality. On the contrary, Maggie is a gorgeous blond in her late thirties with the nicest personality you could want. As her therapy progressed, we discovered she was sexually abused by her brother in her childhood. Only in the last few years had she let herself be aware of her abuse and then only on an intellectual basis. Emotionally she still could not handle the situation. These repressed emotions intensified her natural tendency to be obsessive and compulsive, which is a rigid behavior that negates balance and can block emotional healing. One way her obsessive and compulsive behavior manifested was through her eating habits. In the past she was very restrictive and limiting about her diet. Her different diets ranged from eating any and all desserts, but only until noon, to eating nothing but beef. As Maggie grew in awareness, she realized her unbalanced ways of eating helped her stay unconscious of what was really bothering her. She realized her obsessive sugar binges kept her feeling physically lightheaded and aggravated a yeast infection she has had for years. Her lightheadedness and yeast condition were her ways of staying out of relationships and not confronting the emotional pain caused by her brother's abuse. When she was lightheaded, she didn't have the emotional strength to make good decisions about men or defend her boundaries effectively. When her yeast infection was flaring up, it kept her uninterested in sex and successfully out of any long-term relationships. Obsessing about weight, habits, or other things are wonderful ways we keep from facing the real, pertinent issues in our own selves. The more Maggie obsessed about food and kept her body weak and unbalanced, the less time she had to solve her real emotional issues.

Now Maggie is aware that when she eats too much sugar, the real reason behind her behavior is she wants to be unconscious about something she is feeling. See now can understand that her unbalanced ways of eating are cues for her growth and larger awareness. Maggie now works with balancing her diet to help strengthen herself emotionally, mentally, and physically. She understands more fully how when one part of her is unbalanced it affects her entire life. Now she is more loving and nurturing to herself. Because of her actions to balance all parts of her, she is seeing changes in her personality. She has gone from being submissive to being assertive and protective of her boundaries. Instead of seeking out men who are married or emotionally unavailable, Maggie now consciously chooses men who are into self-growth and communication.

Maggie's experience is a powerful example of how underlying beliefs or energy are like magnets that bring you situations which correspond to your inner beliefs. If you are feeling angry and worthless, you will attract corresponding situations until you heal those emotional wounds inside you. You are not completely in control or balanced in the present until you have healed all your emotional baggage of the past.

So how do you heal the emotional part of yourself? The first step is to acknowledge the emotional side of yourself. Then realize healing is a process and can take some time.

Probably the most important aspect of healing your emotional self is to release ALL judgments about feelings in general. Many people, including me, were taught that if we cry or feel hurt, we are not strong, or if we feel anger, we are not good. When you put judgments on feelings, it limits (and can destroy) the ability to feel what is necessary for you to heal. Love yourself enough to experience any and all feelings. Release all judgments about your feelings, and feel what there is to feel, whether it is sadness, anger, fear, or anything else. This allows you to be fully in the present.

For Emotional Healing

Here are some exercises to facilitate this healing process. Many times it facilitates your healing process to imagine your emotionally wounded self as a child or a baby. It doesn't matter if you remember your childhood or not. What counts here is your honesty with yourself about the feeling(s) you missed, like love or affection. Discover what these feelings might have produced, such as anger.

Get in a comfortable position and sing a high vibratory word. Do this for 10 minutes. Follow with different visualizations of yourself as a baby being held and loved. If you lacked a loving parental figure, see a new one who is totally loving and kind. Feel what the baby would feel and allow any sadness or anger to surface. Imagine a beautiful Spiritual being next to you when you visualize yourself as a baby. See the Spiritual being sending you love from God and telling you that you are worthwhile because you are a part of God or Spirit.

Work with your baby developmental stage until you feel nurtured and safe in your visualizations. Then go on to your next stage as a toddler. See yourself safe and fill yourself with love. At each stage of development of life, give yourself all the emotional support you didn't get from your parents or siblings when you were growing up. Work up until the present time, changing any beliefs you might have absorbed from your parents' belief system that you no longer want. This process may take several weeks, months or longer. Take your time. Know this change is achieved as a process and doesn't necessarily come overnight. (An excellent book that may help you understand more is *Homecoming* by John Bradshaw.) ❧

As you work on your emotional balancing or healing, you might want to seek professional counseling. Give yourself permission to do whatever it takes to claim your emotional self without shame or fear. Not having a fully-functioning emotional self is a handicap; you function and get around, but not as freely as you could if you didn't have the handicap. Be all you can be and learn to love your emotional self. After all, God gave you emotions for a reason.

The Mental Body ❧

Your mental self or body comprises both the conscious mind and the unconscious mind. The conscious mind is the seat of reason and logic. The unconscious mind holds all your habits and deeper programs or beliefs.

To achieve mental balance takes cooperation and understanding. When your mind is in harmony, your conscious and unconscious minds work toward the same objective. Your thoughts can then produce peace and tranquility. When the two aspects of our mind are in conflict, we have trouble reaching our objectives.

Let's say you want to quit smoking. The logical, conscious mind realizes smoking is bad for your health. So you decide to quit, but part of you gets in the way. You keep hearing little messages from your unconscious mind, like "Smoking is my friend," or "It will be too tough to live without cigarettes." Those goal-blocking messages come from your unconscious mind, which has no logic or reason. Your thought process is divided in its objective because your conscious mind thinks one way and your unconscious mind another.

To achieve mental harmony, both parts of your mind have to believe the same thing. Because the unconscious mind has no logic or reason, it keeps the old beliefs until you find a way to change them. The unconscious mind is the more powerful of the two, and even if you want to consciously change, first you must change any unconscious beliefs that are in conflict with your conscious desire. The unconscious mind runs like a computer. It makes no analysis of the information it holds, it just performs. To achieve your objectives, you first have to find what belief(s) the unconscious mind is holding that blocks your progress.

How can you find this out? I tell my clients to look at what is in their lives right now. For example, if you consciously believe you want to be thinner and you have been overweight for a length of time, unconsciously for some reason you feel more comfortable being heavy. This holds true with everything in your life. Whatever is presently in your life represents the true beliefs you hold regarding any particular part of your life, whether they involve money, relationships, health or anything else.

Positive Thinking 🍃

One way to change your unconscious thought processes is to use positive thinking. Consciously monitor the thoughts you create. If they are negative or in conflict with your goal, change them. Only you create your thoughts, so become a master of what you allow yourself to think. The mind needs a gentle awareness, not a firm hand. So when you find yourself off track, gently put your consciousness back on your goal. Consistency is vital for success!

I have discovered mental programming will only take you so far in changing thought patterns. Eventually you have to go above the mind to correct erroneous thinking and tap into your Spiritual self. Remember that the mind, emotions, and body are tools used by Soul to live in this dimension. Soul is in control. The mind is limited by its physical nature so there are limits to its growth and power.

I use positive thinking, but I also get in touch with my spiritual self every day and open myself up to God and myself as Soul. Thus I know all my thoughts are being affected in a profound and most powerful way for my good and the good of all. Contemplations (ways of getting connected to Spirit) definitely help balance your mind in the best direction for your highest purpose. And when you live your life based on Spirit, your lower bodies (your mind, emotions, and physical body) are balanced and affected in the best way possible. The more you know what part of you is out of balance, the easier it is to bring your whole life into harmony.

Actions That Create Balance ❧

Each of your bodies affects the other parts of yourself, your outlook on life, and the actions you take. If one part of your life overshadows another, an imbalance occurs. If you work all the time and don't take time out to rest or to play, you eventually will become unbalanced. This lessens your effectiveness as a person.

To drive home this point, I want to share with you the realizations of Dr. Cindi. Dr. Cindi came to me at her wits' end. She was feeling out of control and exhausted. At her first session she told me she barely had eked out the hour to see me.

During our first session, I found out she never gave herself any free time or did anything to nurture herself. She was constantly giving all her time and energy to her

patients, husband, and children. She was a typical dysfunctional nurturer, accepting all the responsibility of her
business and home life. Dr. Cindi wanted peace of mind
badly. She is an open person and willing to embrace new
concepts. I explained to her the concepts of balance and
self-love. I told her when she took time out for herself to
recharge and have fun, her whole life would prosper. I
emphasized the need for healthy boundaries and releasing
the responsibility for other adults. I then put her through
the hypnosis process to bring these new concepts deeper
into her unconscious.

She came back the next week beaming! During the
space of a week, she set boundaries with her teenage son
and husband and scheduled two half-days off to have fun.
She felt like a new woman. Before, she couldn't even see
how she was going to come for an hour's therapy; now,
because her conscious and unconscious beliefs were coming into harmony, she was aware she could change anything in her life. Week after week, her life continued to
improve. Her business increased as well as her time off.
Her good family relationships got even better. She noticed
how her energy affected everyone in her life. When she felt
balanced and nurtured, she could see more patients and
have a deeper, more satisfying family life. She realized her
energy affected everything in her life, and when she was
out of balance, so was the rest of her life. Before she was a
victim; now she is on the road to mastery!

Balance occurs and is created in the moment. There
are times when it is very right and balanced to work more,
and there are times when it is perfect to play more. I always
ask myself this question to find out what I need for my own
balance and harmony in the present moment: **"What do I
need right now to create value in my life?"**

This question helps me zero in on what I need. Value
to me means allowing me to be all I can be in every cate-

gory of my life. In the higher regard, value also means anything that helps open you to your spiritual self as Soul. So when I ask myself this question, I am taking an inventory of how my day or week is going, and I am as honest as I can be about my progress.

Let's say I've been working very hard and I feel burned out and unproductive. When I ask myself what I need to create value in my life, it helps me focus on my responsibility for my own happiness and well-being. This question helps to put me in the driver's seat to take actions to create my happiness. And when I am happy, it affects others in a positive way, because my energy and vibrations are more positive. Creating value for myself helps me stay out of co-dependency in relationships, because I know it is up to me and no one else to make my own balance and happiness.

I may feel tired and drained because my emotional self needs fun or my physical body needs a rest, or a combination of both. I may not know what I need right away, but if I continue to work hard and not stay in balance, something is going to suffer. I have to take responsibility to find out what I need right now to create balance in my life.

If you don't know what you need, try different actions until something clicks. You will find out more quickly what you need in your life, whether it is rest, play, more work, communication, nurturing, or getting in-touch with your spiritual nature. Without actions, you stay powerless and a victim. **Actions always place you more in being the master of your life!**

There are times when I am not sure what I need for my greatest good, so I go within myself and ask. You will be surprised at how much you really do know about what you need when you ask yourself. Letting yourself know is the beginning of self-awakening. I am amazed when people say they don't know what they need or want in life. If you really don't know, act as if you do. Eventually, you will allow yourself to know. Deep in your Soul you always know the answers, which go beyond logic and reason to pure understanding.

Next, let yourself have what you need. This is usually hard to do. We have been taught to deny our needs. We often believe our needs are not important or we will be better people if we let others have their needs met over ours. Whenever you deny your own growth or needs you will suffer for it, and so will everyone around you. When you deny your needs, you deny parts of yourself. Remember, neglecting any one of your parts is the same as neglecting your whole self. You then live only at incomplete capacity. This diminishes the positive effects on yourself and everyone else.

Mothers usually have a really hard time with this, because they have been programmed to fill everyone's needs before their own. Over time, they really can get out of balance, as Dr. Cindi found out. They neglect their spiritual, emotional, mental, or physical selves and wonder why they feel depressed or are overweight or sick. And when they are depressed, sick, or feeling bad about their bodies, their state of consciousness affects the whole family. The same is true with fathers. Many fathers work too hard and neglect the other parts of themselves. Then they have nothing left to give to themselves, their wives, or their children.

Try to touch base with your inner self a little more often. Give yourself permission to have what you need, whether it's fun or time to rest. You will then become balanced, more capable, and a much happier person.

Giving yourself this permission is important. Without it, you create a life that doesn't allow balance. YOU have to give balance to yourself. It doesn't magically appear.

I have had a hard time giving myself permission to have fun or to take time off. Until recently I worked six and seven days a week. I found myself living a one-dimensional existence. There was a part of me that felt if I didn't work all the time, I wouldn't survive. But I kept asking Spirit to guide me in my growth and to help me manifest my creativity. Circumstances kept presenting themselves in such a way that I had to take more time off. Through this forced time away from work, I realized how important time away was for my health and emotional well-being. I now incorporate more non-work time in my schedule. I make as much income as before, but now I am happier and I have time for my creative endeavors, which include my painting and writing.

Balance in life and within your separate bodies is very individual. Someone may need five hours of sleep and do fine, while you may need ten. You may need to play more than your spouse or you may need more quiet time than anyone you know. Know whatever you need in the present moment to create value in your whole being is okay. Do whatever you need to do to grow toward self-mastery and true happiness. This is what a balanced whole life is all about: your personal journey to your true self. Give yourself permission to take the steps needed for this journey, including creating balance and harmony in all aspects of yourself and your daily life.

The more you ask yourself to have balance in your life, the more you will know how to create it and live it!

Anger

Volcanic energy
hidden from self.
Excess baggage
timed to explode,
Anytime, Anywhere.
In the most unexpected ways.

Children, we're so afraid
to feel,
to acknowledge,
this pent up rage.

Why do you stuff it inside?
Thinking it's not there,
only it is.
Eating away at your life,
your joy,
your health.

Bring it up and out,
Acknowledge it.
Free yourself
from those invisible chains.
Not to harm another,
but to create value
for yourself.
Making a place now
in your life
for love. ❧

Chapter 8

Anger

Part of our growth as Soul is learning how to create value with anger, then transcending the need for it. As much as we may try, we can never transcend anger until we acknowledge it, learn how to constructively release it in the moment, and experience and release all the anger we have repressed from our past. Until we learn how to create value with our anger, it will always affect our lives in negative ways. How is anger affecting your life? If you ask this question and allow yourself to be honest, your answers will emerge. This chapter will help you to identify, process, and understand anger more fully. I think most people are shocked to hear anger can create value or has any value at all. After reading this chapter, I hope you will see your anger in a new light, and see that you can experience it in new ways which will create value for you.

Anger As Energy ❧

Understanding what anger is helps you to deal with it more effectively. Anger is very real energy. As you know, we all are composed of energy. Since energy comes in different shapes and forms, everything you think of as you is energy, including your thoughts, emotions, and physical body.

When you realize anger is very real, as real as physical objects, you are then on your way to greater growth and change, broadening your view of what is real. When you make this shift in awareness to incorporate a greater understanding of life, you can use this awareness to evolve in your personal and Spiritual life.

When we make a shift in our understanding regarding anger, we can take more effective actions. Most of us have had a hard time dealing effectively with or creating value through our anger. Most of us have learned to either suppress anger, or we have released our anger in rageful ways. Suppressing our anger ends up hurting ourselves and being rageful hurts others. So, what other options do we have in dealing with our anger? In the life path of growth, it is important to deal with anger in ways that create value for you and for all concerned. There are healthy ways to deal with anger, such as acknowledging your anger in the present moment and healing old anger issues that you have repressed. Throughout this chapter I will give you effective tools to create value through your anger that you are aware of now and with anger you may have repressed from your past.

Creating Value ⩫

Creating value or worth means doing what is best for your own growth or unfoldment as a human and a spiritual being without infringing on the boundaries of others. Sometimes to others, it may not always appear you're creating value, and that's okay. To truly grow, it is important to do what you feel is right for your life and spiritual self in the present moment, while respecting the boundaries of others. Only you know what is right for you, and as individuals we need different experiences for our personal and spiritual development.

Defending Your Boundaries ⩫

Creating value may mean dealing with your anger in ways others don't always agree with—they may not like the way you handle a situation or express yourself. To deal with your anger in the moment, you may need to communicate your feelings to others. When you communicate your anger to others, it opens the door for love and growth in all ways if you are expressing it to create value. For example, in my life I've had a very hard time accepting and expressing my anger, especially to my family or to people who are close to me. I found it especially hard to tell one of my sisters that she irritated me sometimes. The issues were usually about my boundaries as a person, and sometimes I got angry when I felt she invalidated my feelings.

In my past, I dealt with my anger in a way that did not create value for me. I repressed my feelings and I wouldn't say what bothered me. I even hid my anger from my conscious self. When I handled my anger this way, I felt like a victim and had no feelings of self-worth. My self-worth suffered because I was cutting myself off from self-love when I didn't stand up for myself. In the example of my sister, I knew she didn't realize she was upsetting me. Most people don't know they are stepping on your toes until you tell them, but if you don't tell others what is bothering you, who will? Step by step, I started voicing my anger when I felt my feelings or personal boundaries were being invalidated. I used my energy and my personal power to stand up for myself. When I first stood up for myself with my sister, she criticized me for expressing anger, but I kept defending my emotional boundaries. Since I stood up for myself, I have a better relationship with my sister, and I have better self-esteem and feelings of self-worth.

This is just one example of how acknowledging my anger created value because I defended my boundaries. The very act of defending yourself and your feelings is an act of self-love, because you are refusing to be abused in any way. Self-love is a powerful, internal way to increase one's self-worth. Communicating your anger can be a tremendous growth step. Expressing your feelings is acknowledging another part of yourself; it is being real. When you communicate your anger with others to release the barriers to love, then they have the chance to be real with you. Repressed anger prevents the flow of love to yourself or to others. People may or may not be ready to handle this deeper and more real way of communicating. But, if you never give yourself the chance to be genuine with others, you could miss opportunities with many people who are ready for this deeper relationship.

People will not always understand your internal needs or struggles, and they don't need to understand them. What is important is that you understand what you need and work on what is right for you. This creates value for your life. It's also important that you do not take away anyone else's rights while you are standing up for your own. Most people feel angry when they feel their boundaries have been ignored or violated. Defending your boundaries as an individual is NOT infringing on another person. Defending is not an act of aggression but an act of protection from someone else's aggression. This will be true whether they are aware of their aggression or not.

Beliefs About Anger ❧

Your beliefs about anger and how to express it were formed in your childhood. The more you know how your beliefs were formed, the more comprehensively you can help yourself change. In my family, we learned indirectly and through the direct actions of my parents that we were not allowed to deal openly with the emotion of anger, and that angry people were bad. This affected the quality of my relationships with my friends and how I felt about me. Every time I felt angry, I internalized the feeling of being worthless, when in reality I was being human! When I became conscious that this was caused from past conditioning, I then had some power to change my negative feelings about myself when I became angry.

You also may carry strong beliefs about anger from previous lives. Most of us don't remember our past lives, so deal with your anger in the present moment. Even if you are manifesting anger from a previous life, you can only grow and change in the present moment.

Most of us come from some kind of dysfunctional home and this upbringing generates a tremendous amount of anger. Sometimes you are aware of it, but most often you are not. Many of my clients have great compassion and intellectual understanding about their parents and their upbringing. They realize their parents did the best job they could. They can mentally understand, "My parents were alcoholics," or "There was sickness," or "My parents had bad childhoods, too."

Many people think that understanding why their parents weren't able to give them the nurturing they needed makes everything all right. They think their intellectual understanding should override feelings of anger. My clients are very surprised to learn they need to feel their anger before they can thoroughly heal or release it.

Thinking you can heal an emotional hurt with conscious, intellectual understanding only is like saying, "My body shouldn't hurt after running a marathon because I know how to run." Or it's like a doctor saying she shouldn't get sick because her knowledge of the body will stave off sickness.

What I have discovered in talking to people, in therapy or out, is most of us don't know how to feel and heal our emotional selves. I cannot emphasize this enough: **you cannot heal your emotional self with mental understanding alone**! To fully heal an emotional trauma (past or present), you have to experience your feelings regarding that trauma and not deny that they exist. Conscious feeling and acknowledgment of repressed emotions is what your emotional body needs for healing.

But your inner emotional self can be scared to death to experience anger you feel toward your mom or dad or whomever was your primary caretaker. Your inner emotional self feels that if you get angry at your parents, then they won't love you or take care of you, so you won't survive. (Also, many of us accept the mass conscious belief that states you are a shameful person if you are angry at your parents for any reason.)

If you don't consciously understand your inner negative beliefs regarding anger ahead of time, acknowledging this anger can make you feel unworthy and fill you with guilt. To protect your inner feelings of worth, you learn to repress your feelings of anger or project your anger onto others or into unhealthy ways of living.

Consequently, you never learn to deal with anger honestly in ways that benefit your total growth. The message being played out in your unconscious mind could sound something like this, "After all, my parents brought me into this world and I owe them my life and gratitude." The unconscious messages that keep playing in your head negatively affect everything in your life, because they are some of the fundamental beliefs that run your life. They limit you from being free.

As babies and young children, we have a limitless need for nurturing and attention. Even if there was such a thing as a perfect childhood, I believe the child still would have some anger over not getting enough of what it perceived it needed. So anger over your childhood is quite normal, and this anger is intensified when there is dysfunction in the home.

If you came from a home where the caretakers were not nurtured as children, they probably didn't have the emotional capacity to give you all the love and nurturing you needed as a child. Children learn from the people around them. If the primary caretakers love themselves, their children incorporate their healthy self-esteem. The same is true if the caretakers lack nurturing in their own lives. This lack of nurturing is mirrored to children, who absorb it and feel they created it. **Children interpret any lack as something intrinsically wrong with them.**

This is what happened to me. Because of her illness, my mother could not emotionally nurture me enough. Usually in this case, the child ends up nurturing the parent and repressing the anger. That's exactly what I did. I repressed my anger and it manifested through my bulimia and drug use. Anger is a natural and normal response for not getting what you needed as a child. If I had felt safe to feel and openly express my anger when I was a child, I believe my bulimia and drug abuse would not have occurred. I could have released my anger energy from my life in the moment, instead of projecting it in the distorted ways I did.

Repressing any emotion or dealing with emotions in unhealthy ways keeps you from growing personally and spiritually. Your anger energy is not being expressed constructively when you repress it, which prevents love and acceptance from shining through you as a whole person. Without total self-love, it is impossible to really love anyone else fully or to fully develop yourself in any way. When you deal with your feelings in the moment and acknowledge what you're feeling, you can release any unwanted feelings more quickly and live completely in the present.

Repressed Anger ❧

It is important to identify your anger and learn how to deal with it constructively. Remember everything about you is energy and it can change forms. Repressed anger can show up in your life in physical, mental, or emotional ways.

Chronic sickness or disease can be an effect of long-term repressed anger. For example, almost all ulcers are caused by repressed stress. Most of us accept this, and the medical profession believes this to be true. Take this principle further. Entertain the concept ALL emotions affect the body in some way, in good and bad ways.

If you have a disease or are constantly getting sick, take stock of the events in your past and present. See if you have angry feelings you have been afraid to feel or acknowledge. As a child, I was always sick. When I started to express my feelings in my teen years, my health improved tremendously.

Another sign of repressed anger is depression. Energy has to go somewhere, even if you have been consciously denying its existence. If anger is still there in your makeup, you might experience it as depression. Most depression is anger energy turned inward toward ourselves. Anger kept inside can be destructive emotionally, mentally, and physically.

Being sick or depressed is a less than satisfactory way to live. Even if you are not interested in living a more spiritual life, you can benefit from releasing denied anger. If you want to reach higher spiritual heights, releasing pent-up anger is absolutely necessary!

Whenever you are repressing anger, you are directly causing destruction to yourself, and indirectly it affects others.

Spirit needs a clear vehicle to flow through. The more you become conscious of your hidden anger, the sooner you can process it in healthy ways and begin to love yourself more completely. You then can open your life more fully to be a channel for Spirit and God.

Another sign of repressed anger is self-sabotage. This is hard to recognize, because self-sabotage takes on so many forms. When events in your life keep you from happiness or reaching your goals, they are signs of self-sabotage. Most of the time, you aren't consciously feeling the anger responsible for your behavior.

If any of these things have happened to you over and over again or in any combination, odds are you are repressing anger. Things might seem to "just happen" to you. You keep meeting the wrong kinds of people, and the relationships you develop are destructive or ineffectual. Or you just get sick all the time. Maybe you rationalize how all the jobs you've had never worked out.

Maybe you never finish the projects you start, whether these are school, hobby, or work related. Other self-sabotage actions are detrimental habits like drugs, alcohol, cigarette smoking, exercise to the point of obsession or bodily injury, frequent accidents, and lack of motivation. These are the most common, but definitely not all, ways you can sabotage yourself. The list goes on and on.

If these scenarios sound familiar and you've tried to change them without results, you probably are angry at something or someone (which could include yourself). Some issue(s) in your life is not being dealt with directly. People who deal with their anger this way probably were taught, directly or indirectly, that expressing anger was bad. They may have been punished for feeling anger or showing it, so instead of dealing with anger directly, they deal with their anger unconsciously. They never really confront the issue at hand, and when they deal with anger this way, they end up harming themselves.

Let me give you an example. My bulimia was one of many ways I sabotaged my own life, and it came partly from my repressed anger. In my heart, I was furious at my mother for being sick. I was angry I didn't get the nurturing, love, and attention a child needs. I was never aware of this consciously while I was growing up. My bulimia was an outer manifestation of my internal rage.

We were taught never to show anger, but my anger energy was still there. This energy had to manifest somehow. My unconscious mind picked bulimia to vent my hidden rage, because I couldn't deal with it directly. This way of dealing with my anger was definitely hurting my body and the quality of my life. My bulimia started to go away when I consciously worked on developing my self-worth and confronting my anger.

The more I confront myself and all my hidden emotional issues or beliefs, the more I grow spiritually and the more harmonious my daily life becomes. In my past, I was terrified to face my anger directly. As a teenager and young adult, I would virtually shake from head to toe when I had to tell someone I didn't like something or I was, heaven forbid, angry at them. But instinctively I knew I had to challenge myself to confront people and issues that bothered me, or I would remain a bulimic and emotionally numb for the rest of my life. It took me 14 years to overcome my bulimia, but I did overcome it!

Everyone at one time or another represses anger. Even if you're the kind of person who beats up on people and is openly nasty and critical, what's behind your actions is your hidden anger. People who are openly violent have short fuses because they have not resolved their anger, usually anger from their childhoods. Even when they beat up on people, the aggression and rage do not help them confront their inner child and heal their real emotional wounds. They are reacting instead of healing, and they are probably terrified of really feeling all the anger from the past.

186

Many people unconsciously believe if they feel all their feelings, they will physically die. No one ever dies from experiencing feelings, but many people are killing themselves with all the feelings they repress. People are scared to feel, just the same.

So what do you do with your repressed anger? How do you heal your inner child? How can you be human, deal with your anger, and grow spiritually, all at the same time?

Acknowledging Repressed Anger ❧

The first step in the process of dealing with anger is realizing and acknowledging you are angry. If you cannot acknowledge what you need in order to change, you may never make headway with your growth. The next step is to know there are no perfect people in the human state of consciousness. Anger is only an emotion. Let go of all judgments about what it means. When you let go of judgments about anger, this frees you up to feel it. **Feeling your anger is the only way to process it.** Releasing judgments about your feelings is paramount to your growth and healing. A feeling is just a feeling. It is neither good nor bad, it just is. It's what you do with it that creates value or not.

In your spiritual and personal growth, it can be very powerful to believe whatever is happening to you is perfect. At first this may be hard to understand. When you really understand that whatever is in your life is the next step in your evolution as Soul, then you can drop all judgments and use what is happening to you in a detached, constructive way for your growth. Over the course of your life, this attitude will help you recognize man-made rules or beliefs that are preventing you from embracing your spiritual evolution. All of your experiences and feelings are teaching you something important on your road to God.

As Soul, you always have free will. You can choose to stay a victim, or you can grow. At any moment in time you are either creating what you want or being a victim. There is no in-between. You have to accept and take control of your life no matter what has happened in the past or what is happening now.

It's one thing to understand and process your emotions about your childhood, and it is quite another to languish in blame about your past. People who sincerely want to evolve tackle the past and learn from it. They do any and all emotional work necessary to heal.

To completely heal, you must release blame and anger about your past. Blaming or staying angry is remaining a victim. Taking action to change yourself is being the master of your life. When you understand your life from the highest perspective as Soul, you realize your life experiences, from childhood on, were either effects from past karma or results of present-day choices. So who can you really blame?

Stages of Loss ❧

Now suppose you've realized your repressed anger. Consciously you have decided to deal with your feelings so you can further grow in Spirit. Your next step is going through the stages of loss.

Simply put, the stages of loss are denial, anger, hurt, and resolution. Denial is the act of not consciously admitting to a feeling or an understanding about a particular event. After confronting the situation, the next phase a person goes through is anger. Next come feelings of hurt and sadness. A person can go in and out of denial while experiencing anger and hurt. This process is a flow, not a rigid schedule. All feelings have to be acknowledged and experienced fully in order to come to resolution. When you reach resolution about something you have been angry about, you have released anger on every level. You are then fully in the present.

A former client of mine named George illustrates this point clearly. George is a middle-aged man who was having trouble keeping jobs, even jobs that were below his potential. He had been feeling depressed and had lacked motivation for several years. I had found out that several years earlier he had an important corporate job, and he had been fired unfairly. His lack of motivation and job spiral corresponded to his firing. I deduced he was repressing anger toward that past situation, and his internal anger energy was manifesting as self-sabotage. I explained my theory to George. He understood, and he started the emotional work of going through the stages of loss regarding his job. Learning how repressed emotions were hurting his present life brought him out of denial about his being fired. We next worked on his anger and sadness regarding his loss. After all the emotions were processed, he came to resolution regarding his situation. George realized he was still a worthy individual whether he got fired or not. Eventually he got more and more confidence and motivation and landed a job on par with his skill and expertise.

This is a very real situation were repressed emotions (in this case, mostly anger) kept George from living fully in the moment. He was still carrying around anger about being fired and that kept him from having a full life. Whenever you experience loss of any kind, you have to go through stages of emotional releasing to heal. The time frame for each loss can vary from minutes to years. The more conscious you are of your repressed emotions, the more quickly you can heal.

Processing Your Anger Effectively

Here are some ways to effectively process anger. These methods can be used for any anger situation, repressed or not.

One way to release long-held anger is to write an angry letter about the situation. You **DO NOT** give this letter to the person involved. It is for your processing only. It is for you to be honest with yourself about how the situation affected you.

It is important to free yourself from guilt while you are doing these exercises. Give yourself permission to be as "down and dirty" as you need to be. Remember, your purpose in this exercise is to FEEL, not to judge yourself for the intensity of your feelings or question whether your feelings are appropriate or not. You can't do this exercise as an intellectual undertaking. Really **feel** as a child would. Don't get caught in the trap of saying, "Well, I shouldn't say this, or that's not nice." Use every dirty word in the book if you need to, and get all your emotions out. Feel all the feelings that have been trapped. Then burn the letter or rip it up and flush it down the toilet or whatever feels right to you to do, as a symbolic act of release.

You may have to do this exercise more than once with the same person or situation. That's okay. Do whatever works to bring out all the energy you've been hiding from yourself. ❧

Another effective process to remove deep anger is working with spiritual contemplations. You can use the ones that follow or come up with your own. You are Soul, and you know what you need. Give yourself permission to know.

190

EXERCISE

Releasing Anger Through Light

These contemplations should be done when you will not be disturbed. They take from 10 to 20 minutes. You judge how long you need. You may want to do them longer or shorter, once a day or more. Judge the results, see how you feel and react afterward.

Get into a comfortable position with your feet flat on the floor, body relaxed. Close your eyes and gently focus on the part of your forehead between your eyes. Breathe in, and when you exhale sing a high vibratory word.

Do this for about 10 minutes. Then mentally state you want to process your anger so you can grow as Soul. With this attitude, you are helping change your karma, and the results will be for your highest good.

Next, try several visualizations. First visualize your anger as red energy leaving your heart and body. See and feel it disappearing into Spirit. Feel your heart get lighter. When you feel your anger is gone and you no longer see the red light, replace your anger with love. Replace the red light with white light. Feel the nurturing, healing presence of the white light. Affirm this is what you are as Soul, a being of light and love.

Remember, some people visualize more clearly than others. Do not be discouraged if you do not "see" things in your contemplations like pictures in a movie. Just imagining what something is like and doing it with feeling will produce the same results. Your intentions and feelings create movement and change. Relax and trust your higher self. ✒

EXERCISE

Healing Anger
Through Spiritual Water

Here's another. Imagine yourself walking on a beautiful day. The sun is shining and the birds are singing. You see beautiful sights and hear beautiful sounds. You come across a sparkling stream or river. Take off your shoes and walk in the water. In the water with you is a highly-evolved Soul who holds a basket, sent by Spirit to help you. You feel totally safe and secure. You relinquish all your anger and put it in the basket. You watch as the being dumps the basket of anger into the water and the anger floats out of your sight.

Next let healing energy from the water filter through your whole body. (The water here represents Spirit.) Know you are no longer alone. Feel strengthened spiritually from the water and the presence of the highly-evolved Soul. ❧

EXERCISE

Throwing Anger Away

Another visualization is to see yourself walking to the edge of a cliff. In your hand is a bag. Put all your anger in the bag and add any resistance to getting rid of the anger into the bag also. Close the bag and throw it off the cliff, out of your heart and life. See yourself going into your daily life surrounded by white light. Visualize your life filled with harmony, peace and love. Know this harmony, peace and love surrounds you and is part of you. Affirm its presence in your daily life.

Or visualize trash cans labeled anger. Feel the anger and see yourself putting your anger in the trash cans, until it is gone. When you no longer can see or feel it, have trash collectors come and take it away, out of your life. Immediately feel and surround yourself with love and acceptance. See and feel the white light around you. 🙠

Shifting Your Consciousness 🙠

You can use many scenarios in contemplation. The important thing to remember is to get your vibrations higher and more tuned into Spirit. You do this by singing your word until you sense a shift in your state of consciousness. The shift can be very subtle. A shift in awareness tunes your vibrations to a higher level. A shift can be a reframing of your thought patterns to the higher purpose of life, or it can be the subtle feeling of being protected and connected more strongly to your spiritual heritage. You may hear sound and see light in your contemplations or observe very subtle changes in the way you look at life. Just singing a high vibratory word creates a shift in your inner self, whether you are aware of it or not. If you can't feel a shift, just sing the word of your choice for about 10 to 20 minutes anyway, then do your contemplations. Even if you don't feel a shift at first, do the contemplations consistently. With repetition you will come to know when these shifts occur in your consciousness.

Allowing the Process of Change ❧

Keep in mind that change is a process. The more consistently you work on ridding yourself of old stuff, the more success you will have. You may need to do all of these techniques and more. You may need professional counseling to help you sort out your anger.

Keep working with it, and your life will change. The actions you take create effects, even if you can't see the results right away. The results will manifest if you are sincere and consistent in wanting to evolve as Soul.

The more you consciously work with Spirit for your growth, the more you will recognize everything is part of Spirit. You will become more aware that the right tools and solutions are being sent to you all the time. The more you listen for the answers with all of your being, the faster you grow and solve your problems. There is no problem in your life without a solution.

Reasons We Keep Anger ❧

There are several factors that keep anger trapped. One big, big reason many people can't rid themselves of anger is because of the ego. When you base your life from the ego, your smaller self, it is easy to feel righteous and justified in keeping your anger. Experiencing anger to create value or to protect your boundaries is coming from an attitude and attention of love and growth, rather than expressing anger from the ego or to punish other people for their point of view. There is a vast difference between the two.

Humans experience anger. It's what you do with it that makes all the difference in your growth. Your ego is always struggling to be heard. When you live from your ego, you stay caught in turmoil and situations that keep you at a lower vibration.

The way to higher growth is to always remember whatever is happening to you is perfect. Your life is unfolding exactly as it should to develop your spiritual self. You can choose to look at any situation as garbage or as Spirit trying to teach you. You can hold on to anger for your petty ego's sake, or you can see what this situation is trying to teach you. The choice is yours.

Emotional survival is another huge reason we hold on to our anger. In many cases our inner children learned to survive through keeping anger. It may not be beneficial to your life now or manifest in logical ways, but remember your emotional self is not logical. So here is an exercise to help you confront and transform your anger part.

EXERCISE

Transforming Your Anger Part

Imagine yourself in a beautiful place. It can be outdoors or indoors. Know you are perfectly safe and protected by white light all around you. Go up to the anger part of you. See how it looks. Notice its dimensions and how you feel when you confront this part of yourself.

Next communicate to your anger part how much you appreciate its help in contributing to your survival. Validate its existence. Intellectually this may be hard to do, but understand in some way this part has helped you survive all the dysfunction in your life.

Tell it you now have a new, more important job for it to do, that is not only going to help you survive, but thrive. This new job is self-love. Tell your anger part self-love is the strongest protection you can ever have and you need its help for this transformation.

Next lead your anger part to a beautiful pond filled with sparkling white light, like little stars. Both of you get in the pond. Feel your anger part accepting this new job. When you feel the acceptance occurring, get out of the pond together and embrace. Have the new self-loving part melt into your heart.

Do this exercise in a high vibratory state of consciousness, during contemplation, or play some beautiful music along with your visualization. You may find yourself feeling many kinds of emotions during this exercise. Lovingly accept them all, for they are all teaching you something for your growth. ❧

Anger Keeps You Connected ❧

Another reason we have a hard time releasing anger is because we don't want to let go of something in our lives. Anger always keeps us connected to the things we are angry at. This is subtle and harder to spot, so let me give you some examples.

Suppose one or both of your parents were very controlling. You may now be able to stand up to your parents and live your own life, but you accomplished this mostly through anger. Through your anger you were able to keep your identity. Fundamentally, you used your anger to survive. Your anger was your way to protect your boundaries. The only way you could survive and not let your parents take control was through staying angry. Unconsciously, you may feel there is no other way to be independent.

When you stay at a consistent vibration of anger, you release control of your life to the people or things that make you angry. Your anger keeps you tied to anything you have it focused on. Instead of attaining freedom, you get imprisoned with your anger. You may feel you are independent of your parents, when actually you are emotionally tied to them. You need to go through the stages of loss, about being overly controlled as a child, to break free from their control. Anger is necessary to break through a loss. And not getting what you need as a child is definitely a loss.

But then you need to go on. Feel the sadness and hurt you need to feel after the anger comes up. Then resolve the situation or come to completion with your parents. If you don't finish the stages of loss, you are using energy to hold the loss in your life and you have reduced your freedom to grow.

Another example of holding on to anger occurs in a romantic relationship where one person wants out before the other does. When someone you care about very much has broken up with you, you stay angry at the person because you don't want to let go emotionally. (You won't always realize this is what you are doing.) Anger **always** is a very strong emotional link. You keep the anger about the break-up, because unconsciously you are afraid of losing the other person's love or releasing the relationship.

The Time Frame for Releasing Anger ❧

Coming to terms emotionally and spiritually with anger can be tricky. Your anger may have many layers. Keep at it until you feel at peace. Some situations will need only a little of your time and effort to change; others may take longer. It's taken me years of effort and different methods to release anger from my childhood, but I believe I finally have. I am freer than I have ever been in my life.

For the first time in my life, I am creating my life the way I want it to be. I am no longer carrying around huge, painful chunks of my past. Releasing repressed anger is definitely worth the work!

Until you heal all repressed anger, you are a puppet on a string, bandied about by an internal vision of what you think is true, but what you think is true is just an old movie. Do you want to be led by the past or do you want to take command of your life? Your future is being created by your actions now. What are you creating now?

You need to address your anger to come to the place where, on all levels, there is only love. You cannot have love in your life or become love in the spiritual sense without dealing with all your anger. Be honest with yourself about anger. It is teaching you something. Most often, it teaches us about love. If every time you got angry you asked, "What is my anger trying to teach me?" you could grow faster. Acknowledge all your anger. It is helping you grow toward love!

Guilt and Fear

Trapped in the passages
of time,
they lay hidden,
festering and black.
Body and mind
unable to heal,
what insidious
creations.
Death to all growth
and love.
We are our own
captives.
We are our own
prisoners.
Only we have the key
to freedom.
Only we can pardon
ourselves! ❧

Chapter 9

Guilt and Fear

Guilt and fear hamper your growth as an individual in every way—physically, emotionally, creatively, and spiritually. You can live without guilt and fear or at least greatly reduce their effects and power in your life. The less you live your life based on guilt and fear, the stronger, happier, and more loving you can be. Remember, you always have choices in how you can create your life. You can have a life dictated by uplifting conscious desires or a life hampered by unconscious limiting emotions. The choice is always yours. If you want to eliminate or reduce the hold these negating emotions have over you, please read on.

Guilt ❧

Guilt and its stronger counterpart, shame, are developed in childhood. Guilt, in essence, is the feeling you get when you perceive you have done something wrong. Shame is feeling in the depths of your being that you are the mistake. Guilt and shame are learned through the interaction of the modeling you receive from the time you were born to the time your reasoning ability is in place. (Most psychologists agree reasoning ability is fully formed by the age of seven to ten.)

During the time you are developing your reasoning ability, you are the most unconsciously suggestive. You learn very directly, and all the information is taken very quickly and deeply into your unconscious mind. From birth until age three or four, you have few personal or mental boundaries as an individual. You deeply absorb all that happens to you from your interactions with others. You don't have full conscious understanding that most of what you are learning is someone else's behavior, not yours. At this time, it is hard for you to separate yourself from others. Consequently, if you are surrounded by other people whose actions promote or teach guilt, you readily adopt those beliefs. Later in life, it becomes natural for you to feel guilty in situations that resemble what you were taught as a child. The beliefs you hold are from past programming that you didn't consciously choose in the first place. For this reason, you aren't totally using free will.

In childhood, the process of accepting feelings of guilt takes place in your unconscious. Your beliefs of what you should feel guilty about get reinforced by the actions and teachings of authority figures and institutions, from teachers, peers, social norms, and religious upbringing. What you may think of as right or wrong is really based on your upbringing. Whatever beliefs you directly or indirectly accepted as a child are reinforced by similar circumstances in your present life.

Until now, you may have automatically accepted what you feel guilty about from the beliefs of others, but **everything** is a belief, and you have the power to believe **ANYTHING** you want. You do not have to hold on to any way of thinking just because you were raised that way or because someone else tells you this is the "right" way to be. Releasing guilt helps you become the master of your own life!

Harboring guilt keeps you from experiencing life and situations you may need as Soul. When you free yourself from the restraints of guilt, you open yourself up for new experiences that you have previously denied. As you let go of behavior created by guilt, other people may not understand or accept your life, your responses, or your reasons for needing certain experiences. You are the one that needs to validate your life and worth. Only you can give yourself the permission to live your life the way you need it to be. The more you buy into guilt, the more you live from other people's points of view of how the world should be and what is right. Their beliefs may be perfect for them, but not for you. This is what you need to remember. By releasing guilt, you give yourself freedom to be you!

It takes courage to stand independent of the crowd. This is exactly what you do when you refuse to feel guilty. You release the limiting chains around your own life that interfere with your growth as Soul. The first step in being your own person is to do what your heart tells you to do. Releasing guilt from your heart is a phase of your independence. This makes more room for love that is inherent in life.

Buying Into Guilt ❧

So much of our lives are lived on "automatic." A lot of us have been trained to be polite and obliging when family members want our time or when friends or associates want us to do something. Many of us have a hard time asserting ourselves. Saying "no" when we don't want to do something or when we don't have the time to do something for someone else is almost unknown to many of us. If you do something you don't really want to do because you feel guilty, you will end up feeling resentful and angry. You feel this way because you are going against what creates value for you. (If you REALLY want to do the things requested of you, this is another matter. Then you are creating value, because you are in total agreement with the request.)

There are people out in life who are on committees they don't want to be on and running errands they don't want to do, but they do them anyway out of guilt. Every time you do something out of guilt or harbor guilt in your life regarding some action you have taken, the more you are being controlled by guilt and the less you are living the life you could be. Your life is being controlled in the present when you react from the unconscious beliefs you absorbed as a child.

Many people trap themselves in the realm of how others think they should live. **You can choose to live freely.** You can live a life perfect for you and in the process grow incredibly, instead of living a limited existence dictated by others' values or beliefs. You can achieve the life you want by releasing and refusing to accept guilt and all its trappings.

For example, I was raised to believe marriage was for life. My mother and father did not believe in divorce, and the Catholic church taught divorce was not in God's plan. The seeds for guilt surrounding divorce were already planted in my unconscious mind when I got married the first time. I believed in staying married for life no matter what happened.

During the harder times in my previous marriage, I fleetingly thought of divorce, but I kept letting my guilt run my life. I believed I was responsible for Greg's happiness, and that I had to stay married to him forever, no matter what. These beliefs were ruling my existence, and my growth as a person was stagnating. I was in therapy during this time, but even with the help of therapy, I couldn't be honest with myself. I was too afraid I might leave my husband if I were really honest about what I needed as a person. Part of me was aware of what was transpiring, but I chose to ignore my need to leave my marriage. Guilt was the biggest reason I stayed with Greg as long as I did.

When I broke through the barriers of guilt, I realized it was best for me and Greg to split up. (Greg also came to that realization, and we are still friends today.) If I had let guilt rule my life, I believe I would still be married to Greg, and my growth I have experienced since would have been stalled, or maybe never attained in this lifetime. Instead, I followed my inner voice of what was right for my life. I realized I was not responsible for anyone else's life, not even my husband's. No one can live another person's life or another person's values. I had to come to terms with my responsibility regarding Greg.

Now, I am not recommending that everyone who is unhappy in marriage chuck it and move on. What I am proposing is that people honestly look and see if their actions are out of guilt and the "shoulds" as I call guilt, or if they are living as the true masters of their destinies and directors of their lives. You answer this for yourself. It may take months or years of Soul searching. Give yourself time, and love yourself through any difficult decision or process you may confront.

Repressed Guilt 🌿

You can also harbor guilt in your body and not realize it. Guilt can manifest as sickness or other physical disorders. This may be harder to spot. If you find yourself sick, ask yourself if you are harboring guilt. Let yourself be honest, and the answers will come to you.

Guilt is energy, as is anger, and when guilt manifests in your body, it has been in your thinking for a while. Your body has the densest energy of all parts that compose you as a person. So when symptoms or sickness arise in your body from guilt, your issue with your guilt is either very intense or of long standing. Basically, guilt energy is trapped in the denser energy that makes up your body.

Let me give you a very powerful example of repressed guilt I encountered with a client. This client came to me to lose about 20 pounds. As with all my clients, I asked for a detailed personal history.

205

This client was a woman with a weight problem that started five years earlier. She had never before had a problem with weight. This was significant, and I wondered what might have occurred five years ago to trigger her weight gain.

As she recapped her life, she told me she had had an abortion. I asked her during counseling if she felt any guilt over the abortion. She said she didn't because she needed the abortion to save her life. I could tell she honestly didn't feel any conscious guilt. So I proceeded in each session to try to change her habits regarding food and exercise.

After several sessions, she still didn't lose weight, though she was eating right and exercising. She should have been losing weight if there was no emotional problem involved. Once again I went back over her history and approached the subject of her abortion. This time I got more details, details that incorporated beliefs from her childhood. She told me she was raised in a fundamentalist religion. I asked her about the religion's belief regarding abortion, and you can guess what her answer was! The church strictly forbade abortion, and its teachings were laden with guilt and shame.

I felt she was hiding guilt from herself that showed up as self-punishment in the form of body fat. The timing of her weight gain was also in accord with my theory: she had the abortion about the same time she started gaining weight. I told her I was going to give her some suggestions in hypnosis that would help her release her unconscious guilt. Her unconscious mind would work with her conscious desire to lose weight, and then she would reach her goal.

The next week she reported she had lost five and a half pounds. She hadn't changed her eating habits or the amount of exercise she was doing. She then realized how powerful thoughts and emotions were in her life and how she could punish herself without being aware of it.

To change the mental and emotional processes of guilt to ones of love and positive self-acceptance, you have to come to an understanding that **ALL** guilt is self-punishment. It limits you from receiving love from others, yourself, and Spirit. It is a negating way to be, and it is most definitely **not** a way to help yourself grow. Guilt uses your emotional, mental, or physical energy to stop you from being open and happy. Guilt negatively affects every level of your being.

All aspects of yourself and the forms of your energy can change. If you can picture energy as either open and expansive or closed and restrictive, then you may get a clearer idea of what you are doing when you allow guilt in your life. Guilt is restrictive in nature. The qualities of this emotion are of limitation and closure. Love, on the other hand, is expansive and limitless in nature.

EXERCISE

How Guilt Feels

For you to get a clearer idea of the qualities of these two emotions, just try this little experiment. First feel and picture, if you can, what it is like to fill your heart with love. Take a few minutes and really feel this love. It maybe helpful to feel the love you may have for a mate or a friend or even your pet. Just be with the love. Notice how your body feels and observe any movement of energy.

You will probably find your heart feeling warm and open and expansive in some way. Openness is expansiveness. Immediately after you have examined your state of energy with love, bring up something that elicits guilt in you and think about this with focused intention for a minute. I bet it takes no time at all to feel the difference between the two energies. How did your heart feel with the guilt? Light and expansive or heavy and dark? With love, did you feel like you could be open and positive? How did your body feel? Did it feel energized and vibrant or closed and heavy? Most people can clearly distinguished the two states. ❧

This was just a short experiment. Imagine what guilt energy does to your body when you hold it for a length of time! The more you clear yourself of guilt and understand the true effects guilt places on your whole being, the happier and healthier you will be.

Guilt as Manipulation ❧

The use of guilt is pervasive. People have used it for centuries to manipulate others to do what they want. Religions and governments have used it to keep people from being independent, keeping them from true growth. Guilt is abusive when used by anyone as a tool of manipulation. When you use guilt to manipulate others, you want to have power and control over them.

An argument for guilt has been that if people didn't feel guilty, they would become savage and world chaos would result. I believe this would not happen, because I feel the basic nature of people is an inner drive to know themselves as Soul, a drive toward giving and receiving love. There will always be people who break laws—this is a given. Everyone is at a different state of development, and some Souls learn their lessons in terrible, hurtful ways, no matter what. But I believe the vast majority of the human race wants to grow and be happy. I feel if people like you and me release ourselves from guilt more often, we can open ourselves to new experiences that are good for us. With our happiness and new expansive lives, we can help others grow.

Fear ❧

Fear is another emotion that restricts your life. It restricts your actions and happier emotions. It restricts your blood vessels and physically affects your body. Fear is not an emotion most people willingly confront or desire to keep in their lives. But you may be experiencing more fear than you realize. Stress is such a common part of our lives, but it is really a mild form of fear. This may surprise many of you, but stress in your body is a physiological result of fear.

Mechanics of Fear ❧

Fear is basic to being human, and it helps you survive. Instinctively, you respond to threats through the "flight or fight" syndrome. It is instinctual, and it is passed down to us from our primitive ancestors who continually experienced and responded to life-and-death situations. At times of perceived danger, the body releases more adrenalin into your bloodstream. The added adrenalin helps your body respond quickly and more effectively to help you out of danger.

Primitive humans used their bodies to ward off attacks, and the physical activity balanced and used the added adrenalin. In these modern times, physical threats to our lives are not as obvious. Today, society encourages nonviolent behavior. Though modern living affords many opportunities to feel threatened, unlike those of our primitive ancestors, the threats are not always physical or the circumstances such that a person should fight back physically. This results in excess adrenalin, because we are not physically using our body to ward off the attacks, and excess adrenalin can make us feel stressed out.

The "life-threatening" occurrences of our daily lives now are things like coming up short on monthly bills, confronting rush hour traffic, or trying to escape the old patterns of thought or negative ways of living. These seemingly non-threatening things cause much stress and unconscious fear.

Perceived Danger ❧

In modern life, most experiences with fear or stress are coming from PERCEIVED dangers. Change or perceived danger create stress, and stress keeps you from experiencing love, peace, and growth to new horizons. You can eliminate a great deal of stress by effectively handling your beliefs, your thinking, and your emotional processes. It is not what happens to you that causes fear, but how you perceive and interpret situations with your thoughts and emotions.

Caryn, a former client of mine in her mid-forties, is a graphic example of how changing perceptions can create a new life. When Caryn first came to me, she said she felt unmotivated, uncaring about life, and tired of everything. She wanted to sleep all the time. Caryn said she felt like she was putting on a mask for society to see, hiding her true feelings and view of herself. She said she saw everything as a threat. But Caryn was open to new teaching and was ready to change.

Well, right away, I started to reeducate her unconscious thinking process about guilt and anger from her childhood, giving her permission to feel long-repressed feelings. At the same time, I taught her about the higher spiritual concepts of life and self-love. Fear of rejection, of not being loved, was at the core of her problem. So we did inner child work on unconditional love and self-acceptance. Within two months, she felt like a different person.

At her last session Caryn related how her life had been for the last few weeks. She said she felt "cozy in her skin, warm and good, and no different than other people." She also stated that she felt at peace with herself, and her fear of people was gone. She appreciated others as "beings of light" and did not get entangled in their negativity. Her husband noticed a change in her and loved her emerging new self. She commented, "Without fear you can love someone better and accept their love and feelings." Caryn also said, "I felt the change that took six or seven weeks with you would have taken six or seven years someplace else."

Caryn's comments are typical of the feedback I get from clients all the time. The ones who are honest with themselves and ready to grow, like Caryn, accept new teachings more deeply and more readily. The basic point here is that changing your perspective about life and what is real does affect every part of your life for the better.

A Different Perspective 🐚

Much of your perceptions about what is dangerous has been created from cultural programming. By the way you were raised, you formed beliefs about what to be afraid of. For example, people of primitive cultures have very different beliefs of what to be afraid of than you do. Much of what you consider permanent and dangerous can be changed by changing your thoughts and by allowing yourself to view life from a different perspective, just like Caryn!

I want to share a story my great friend Beth told me to illustrate this point in a different way. One Sunday we were at her house on the deck doing what we do best together—talking! It was one of those outstanding Indian

Summer days; the leaves were perfect and the temperature was warm and balmy.

Beth has a cute little dog named Huey, and we were watching Huey play with his favorite toy, a little red ball. As we were throwing the ball to Huey and talking, Beth had a great flash of awareness about fear and how it restricts your life. You see, Huey is a big chicken when it comes to walking up or down steps. He is a little dog, and steps pose a big problem for him. He doesn't like to go down the steps alone and when his ball rolled down the deck steps and into the back yard, Huey was frightened. We observed Huey trying to figure out how to get that ball without going downstairs by himself. Huey kept looking at Beth, "asking" her to carry him or get the ball for him, but Beth stood firm. She wanted Huey to conquer his fear.

Beth said Huey's fear reminded her of people when they are afraid to change or try something new. People want this "new thing" in their lives but are afraid to leave the old familiar surroundings to get it. They are paralyzed and may even try to have someone else take responsibility for them because they are afraid to do it themselves. What seems so frightening is really just little steps to a new awareness or to the prize which you seek. What holds you back is not the situation, but the perceived danger involved in the new step to growth. **Most of what you fear is illusion!**

Beth finally gave Huey a helpful shove down the first step, and he managed the rest himself. Once Huey got down the steps he became engrossed in the back yard. Because this was a new experience for him, he started to sniff around and soon he lost interest in his ball. He found himself comfortable and happy in these new surroundings!

Beth observed if you can just take the first step into a new thinking or action, before you know it you will find yourself fully participating in this new way of living. It soon feels fun and comfortable. When you can overcome the barriers that keep you from the little red ball in your life, you find your fear about the new experience was an illusion!

Taking Action ❧

Fear and guilt can restrict you from love and experiences of growth, and guilt and fear can create barriers to deeper relationships. Fear prevents your heart from opening with love for others because you feel unsafe to be yourself. Guilt limits the way you live your life, restricting what is possible for you to experience. If you want to rid yourself of fear and guilt, the first requirement is sincerity of your desire, backed by consistent actions, changing those old patterns and beliefs of fear and guilt.

You can sit around all day long and think you want to change, but if you don't take action, you stay in your victim role. **Actions speak louder than words!** You need to want to change with the same intensity and commitment as a person who is dying of thirst wants water. The person is not only thinking of water, but will do anything to get it. To change your life and evolve into higher states of awareness you must have this same kind of desire, and back it up with committed actions. Then you will not be dependent on anyone telling you how to live. It is up to you to find what you need. Your inner self or Soul will direct you to the right vehicle, which will be perfect for your growth at that time in your life. The growth or change you seek is an ongoing process, but even a journey of a thousand miles begins with the first step. If you never act to change, you will never reach your destination.

Please feel free to use these suggestions. As your consciousness and your spiritual vision expands, the tools you used before may take on new meaning. Or if you find that nothing here helps you, experiment with other tools and ways for your growth. The stronger your desire to change, the faster you will find the tools to accomplish change. Be assured you can release old thought patterns that no longer serve you. It takes your actions combined with sincerity to do this.

All these exercises can be used to release guilt or fear. Use them when you want to change or release either emotion. As with any exercises in this book, keep in mind you may have to do them for a length of time. Also, they can be even more powerful in combination with other techniques, courses, or therapy. No one tool is effective for all cases.

Consistency in your actions regarding changing your life is of utmost importance. Without consistent actions, no change will occur. Be open in your life to all vehicles that will help you grow.

EXERCISE

Releasing Fear and Stress

When you want to rid yourself of the emotional hold of fear or stress, accentuate the particular feeling even more, face it, and understand you can let it go. Releasing like this shows you, consciously and unconsciously, that you have power over it. Do this exercise when you are quiet, alone and in a place where you can focus safely on the feeling. Let's say you are dealing with feeling fearful over not having enough money or some other situation. Bring up the fear even more. Feel it more intensely on purpose. This puts you in control, being the master of your life. You have power over feeling out of control with fear. After you intensely bring up this feeling, breathe deeply from your abdomen several times. Every time you exhale, release the fear. Releasing is the process of using breathing and thoughts to consciously let go of something. Your imagination, along with deep breathing techniques, can facilitate your letting go of the particular belief or feeling you want to release.

When fear gets trapped in the body, you feel stressed out. Deep breathing from your lower abdomen is especially effective in helping release emotional energy from your body. After you have brought up the feeling and released it, do this same thing several more times. With each confrontation with your emotion, be more courageous. Intensify the fear freely, so you can release even more of it. Remember, you can not release or change anything in your life if you cannot fully **confront** it.

Each time you exhale, say to yourself, "This is just a feeling and it is no big deal." Reaffirm you have the personal power to be in control. When you are speaking to yourself in the contemplative state, **ALWAYS** think and talk to yourself positively and in the present tense. Your unconscious mind knows only the present and it does not understand negatives. If you say, "I will not be fearful anymore," the unconscious mind registers, "I will be fearful."

Never communicate to your unconscious mind in the future tense. If you put your expectations in the future, this is where the unconscious mind will leave them—somewhere in the future. If you want something, bring up feelings as if what you want is being achieved right now.

After you have confronted your fear and released it, reframe your thinking. (Reframing your thinking means putting a particular situation in a different light.) For example, maybe your car was hit and you are afraid of what the bills will be to fix it. A reframing of this situation could be thinking you are happy that you are physically well after this accident, or thinking you might have needed work done on your car anyway, and now your insurance will cover it. You are constantly reframing without realizing it! But now you can be a conscious creator in reframing, which keeps you at cause in your life and helps you stay more peaceful and harmonious. ❧

EXERCISE

Replacing Fear with Light

For this exercise, surround yourself with a calm, peaceful feeling and light. Pick a soothing color, such as blue. Focus on the color and imagine that where your fear had been is now filled with this color and a beautiful feeling of peace.

For all these exercises, it is best before beginning to take 10 or 15 minutes and get in a high vibratory state by either singing a high vibratory word or listening to soothing music. Listening to music and singing high vibratory words lift your vibrations higher than the pattern of energy in your daily life. ❧

Gaining a New Perspective

Try this exercise when you want to gain a new perspective on anything in your life. If you feel guilty or powerless in a situation or with another person, just imagine yourself leaving and floating above your body. Look at yourself, looking at your situation.

As you float above your body, see the situation as objectively as you can. If you are allowing yourself to feel guilty about someone or if you are stuck in old patterns with people and you want change, see your situation in a new perspective. When you are "above" your body, see yourself as responsible for your life. See the higher truth of the situation and let your higher self give you the new perspective and objectivity you need. You stop your growth many times because you fail to get above your old thinking. You cannot change old patterns with old thinking. This exercise helps you open up new ways of looking at something, helps you get a new and higher perspective.

When you feel an internal shift in the way you think or feel about a situation, come back down to your body and bring the new perspective into yourself and the situation. Though you have just become consciously aware of the new perspective, it has always been a part of you. Realize that you have to open up to this higher way of seeing and living life. The understanding is always in you. **Give yourself permission to know**. Then **give yourself permission to act** on what you know. ❧

EXERCISE

Throwing Away Guilt or Fear

Another exercise you can do after you have raised your vibrations is to see yourself at the top of a beautiful staircase that has 20 steps. Surround yourself with white light or any color light that makes you feel strong and protected. Blue, violet, gold, pink and white are all of a high spiritual vibration and, consequently, you probably will get the best results with these colors.

Visualize holding in your hand anything you may feel afraid of or guilty about. Make those things in your hand VERY tiny. Look at them. Pick them up and examine them. Doing this helps you realize you can handle anything in your life.

When you no longer feel attached to being afraid or guilty about these things, then throw them away. Intensify the light and feel yourself as strong and loving. Walk down the stairs with this new confidence and strength. (Walking down the stairs helps you to create the new image of yourself deeper into your unconscious mind.) At the bottom of the stairs look at yourself in a full length mirror and really like what you see. ❧

Keep working at whatever guilt or fear comes up in your life. You do not have to continue living with old negating thinking and feeling patterns. The more actions you take to change the way you think about guilt and fear, the faster you become the master of your life. Don't let your old ways of living master you!

Values of
the Higher Self

When we live our life
from rules and wants
of the little self . . .
the results of such,
ensnare our light within.

As we evolve,
and live from the light
of what can be . . .
this day,
becomes elevated for all to see.

Kindness and love to share.
These are the new rules to live by;
our new life, our new awareness,
abundant with the warmth of love
and light
endlessly, timelessly, now! ❧

Chapter 10

Values of
the Higher Self

This chapter discusses ways of living and thinking for your greater spiritual advancement. These values, the higher aspects of living, affect all aspects of your life. These values are ways of thinking and acting that help you get in contact with yourself as Soul. I invite you to experiment and learn how these values affect your quality of life and inner connection with Spirit and God.

In each moment, you choose how to live, and the choices you make affect your life. With each action you take you are telling life who you are and where you are going. The causes you make with your actions create who you are in each moment. Whether the actions you make in your life are judgments, thinking patterns, or physical actions, they are consistently creating who you are. So your actions either raise or lower your vibrations or consciousness—you either open yourself to Spirit or move away from connecting with Spirit.

Now, I am not telling you to live any certain way. I definitely believe each person grows in the way that is best for him or her. This chapter is intended to help you uplift your awareness and speed your spiritual growth no matter what path you have chosen. Everything in this book encompasses a process of living. Consistency of your total actions, not just your intellectual understanding, is key to your growth in the spiritual realms as well as in the physical ones.

Know that no awareness or change is achieved overnight. The more you allow yourself to change with love and acceptance, the deeper and more real the change is.

Detachment &

Many spiritual leaders talk about detachment as an important perspective to acquire for your highest growth. The idea of detachment is very misunderstood. Detachment, simply stated, is living from a state of awareness in which whatever happens in your life is okay. By "okay," I mean you realize whatever happens to you creates the perfect circumstances for your growth as Soul. When you live from this detached state you let go of internal ego or emotional struggle as to how things in your life have to be. All the "shoulds" and the "have-to-be-this-ways" fall away from your ego and thinking. It is a state of awareness where Spirit guides your life, instead of your ego telling you what to do. It is a way of working with the highest powers instead of your small, limited human ego. Detachment is a state of consciousness in which you live with the awareness that all things change and when you don't get the things your ego wants, or circumstances are different than what you're wanting, you find it is no big deal.

With a detached attitude you can enjoy life more fully, because your consciousness is more fully in the now. You are less concerned with what is or isn't in your life at the present moment. Living from a more objective viewpoint, you become less **attached** to daily life around you. When you are not as immersed in the things or the circumstances around you, you don't suffer when things don't go as you planned. Detachment is a state of mind and Spirit. You realize all the things in your life, except Soul and Spirit, are not permanent. You enjoy what there is to enjoy and feel what there is to feel, but you are grounded to the core of your true self as Soul. You "go with the flow" of your life, without becoming swept away over change in your present circumstances.

Detachment—Focus On Spirit ❧

With detachment, you are aware everything on Earth will pass on, change or die. Detachment keeps you focused on the true purpose of life, your Soul's growing toward God. Your daily life is a drama to teach your Soul what it needs. The less you are attached to the material outcomes of your life, the more you can grow in Spiritual awareness. Detachment is making Soul the controlling aspect of your life, not your ego. Detachment can be difficult to attain because your ego constantly tries to control you. Your will constantly tries to get its own way.

If you understand Spirit forms everything we know of as life, then you know Spirit is more powerful than your ego. Spirit always exists. Your ego and will are from the physical realm, and their nature is limited.

What we usually do everyday as people is put our ego and will above Spirit, and when we live life this way we become very attached to outcomes. We want things to go the way our ego or our emotions want them to go, or we focus on the comforts of the physical body. When you live your life strictly from ego you have more suffering and your actions are not for your highest ultimate good.

Attachment Leads to Pain ❧

Attachment to things and circumstances leads to pain, because all life is change. Pain comes because we want transitory things to always be in our lives. Unconsciously (or consciously) we think they will fulfill us.

This doesn't mean you can't feel deeply for people or enjoy life, or that you can't have goals. Your greatest lessons are to be had in the present. To deny your present reality is escapism or denial. I believe detachment is a marriage of the material world and the Spiritual. Your actions should be directed from your highest self, not one that is limited. When you do this, detachment is achieved, and at the same time, you can live a full physical life.

Part of living a full physical life encompasses making goals. The detached way of making goals is to ask Spirit to bring whatever is best for your deepest good and the deepest good of others. Let go of any strong energy or attachment to what you want. You will always get what is the best for your highest growth when you create goals in this manner. Remember, Spirit is always on your side.

When you live from the consciousness of detachment, you let Spirit guide you. It is being of the world yet not part of it. Live fully and enjoy what there is to enjoy. Know the drama of this life is not you, it is a dream. The real you is Soul!

Attachment Affects Outcome

A good example of how attachment to an outcome can negatively affect your life is what happened when I met my first husband, Greg. At that time I was just becoming aware of personal power in my life, and I was mostly using my personal power from the attached state of my ego. I used positive thinking then in ways to try to control situations, people, and circumstances. I thought the best thing for us was to get married, and I used my will and energy to make it happen.

Well, Greg did ask me to marry him even though he still had many doubts about getting married. These strong doubts were not about his love for me but whether it was right for him as an individual to get married at that time.

Because of my **attachment** to being married and the intense energy I placed on this situation, I persuaded him to go through with the marriage. (I do realize I am not responsible for his decision, but all things are energy, and energy affects life.) I was VERY attached to the outcome of his decision and I did not give it to Spirit and ask for my higher good. Instead, I was coming from what my ego wanted, so I feel my attachment did affect his decision.

We eventually got married, but we weren't happy. Greg was unhappy because he felt he had unfinished business regarding his own growth and his unhappiness affected me. If I had let Spirit guide me, I believe the outcome would have been different and the hard lessons I learned through the marriage might have been lessened.

Detachment Leads to Growth ❧

I did not force my will on Paul, even though it hurt me very much when he broke our engagement. I stayed detached, and to the best of my ability allowed Spirit to guide my life for my highest good, though at the time what was for my highest good wasn't very clear to me. I feel because both Paul and I practiced detachment about the outcome of our relationship, not only did our marriage manifest, but it manifested in the most perfect way for our growth as individuals. We needed to heal our inner issues apart from each other to have a strong marriage. Our separation turned out to be the shortest route for our individual happiness and our happiness as a couple.

Now I try to use my ego and will in conjunction with Spirit. I realize I truly am Soul and I want to be the most conscious, most highly evolved person I can be. Spirit, the forming energy of life, is here for my good and I am learning to trust Its guidance.

One way to help yourself let go of attachment and the pull of your ego is to do some form of spiritual exercise each day. Ask for guidance from God or Spirit to learn and be shown whatever you need for your spiritual growth. When you start each day this way, you discover that working with Spirit is a lot easier than with your pure will. You will be lead to answers and develop in ways your will or ego could not even imagine. When you work with Spirit you work with the forming stuff of all of life and your attachments of how things have to be drop away.

As I have allowed and trusted Spirit to use me as a vehicle, my life has opened up incredibly—spiritually, personally, emotionally, and financially. The basic, fundamental aspect of Spirit is abundance and joy. The more you come from dedicating your actions as a vehicle for Spirit, the more you are guided to your highest good. The less you are attached to results your ego wants and the more you realize that whatever is happening to you is PERFECT for your growth and happiness, the more peaceful and happy you become. Trust and peace start to develop when you live your life from this active state of detachment. Detachment does not mean you are a victim. It does not mean releasing your power in creating what you want in your life. Detachment is truly an active state where you know and feel your partnership with God and Spirit.

Non-Interference ❧

Another aspect of living in a detached way is to let go of control of others, or non-interference. Many times, whether you are aware of it or not, you live your life trying to control other people. You may do this in direct or subtle ways.

Trying to change others and force your beliefs or your way of living on them is interference. It's getting into other people's space and trying to direct them, such as telling them how they must feel or manipulating them through guilt. When you do this, you interfere with their rights as Soul to be the way they need to be (even if the what they are choosing is to consciously or unconsciously be a victim). All of us have the right to live life the way we need to if we don't interfere with anyone else's rights.

This doesn't mean you can never make suggestions to help people. Interference comes into play when you have an **attachment** to the outcome of your suggestion, when you force your will or energy into their space. Sit back and think about this. How many times have you given suggestions and your energy or intent was attached about having a situation go your way? How many times have you been intent on someone doing something they didn't want to do because you absolutely knew they had to "for their own good"? This is attachment.

This lesson can be hard to learn. Many times you care so much about someone that you interfere with their lives. Your ego thinks it knows what is best for this person's growth. You are interfering when you force your energy on someone to change. Your ego is attached to the results and thinks its way is the only way. The grosser form of interference is physical abuse; subtler forms of interference involve the use of your energy from your emotional self or mind. As you become more aware and conscious, you will see subtler and finer examples of interference. As you become less attached to how other people should live, your life blossoms.

One of the benefits of becoming more awakened to how life works is discovering that you can consciously take actions to create more harmony, balance, love, and joy. Letting go of interfering in other people's lives is a giant step to creating harmony in your life!

Interference happens many times when you think you are actually helping. When you take responsibility away from others you help them stay victims. This is what happens in co-dependent relationships. Remember, it's not that you can't give suggestions to others; it's your **attachment** to the other person doing what you suggested that causes interference. Put very simply, you are trying to control another Soul. This can be very hard at times to keep in perspective. By letting go of interfering with someone's thoughts and life, you will create only positive changes in your life.

For example, I would be interfering as a therapist if I were so attached to the outcome and potential growth of

227

an individual that I abused my power as a counselor. I would be interfering and controlling if I forced a client to stay in therapy longer than he or she wanted to. The force could be no more than a strong suggestion that had my energy attached to it. I would be taking responsibility away from them. Interference can be badgering your mate to quit smoking, or constantly telling someone how to do something because you think it is the only right way to do something. Interference can be subtle or blatant.

Find out what ways you may be using your energy to interfere or step over other's boundaries. The more your consciousness grows, the more you become aware of personal boundaries and how you may be interfering with others. Allow yourself to discover ways you stop your growth through interference.

For example, how often have you had an opinion and thought another person wrong or stupid just because he or she didn't agree with you? How often have you tried to change the other person's mind to what you considered right? This is interference. How you use your energy causes interference or not. Only you know if you are consciously interfering in another's personal space or boundaries, their thoughts or personal beliefs. Also, when you are being interfered with, it is your right to stand up for yourself and protect your personal boundaries.

Interference Through Prayer ❧

You are even interfering when you pray to change someone in any way, if you do not have their permission to do so first. This is true even if they are sick. If you have permission to pray for someone, structure the prayer and your energy regarding the person's welfare so you let God and Spirit do what is best. You must be careful not to be attached to the outcome.

There are many situations where you may want to help another person or to pray for them. I think one of the hardest things to do is not do something for someone when the person is living like a victim, or not to pray for recovery when the person is sick.

When my father was dying of cancer, I had to stop myself from praying for his recovery. I gave it to Spirit and I asked for his highest good to manifest. Living may not of been for his highest good as Soul.

This may sound strange, but each individual has to learn what they need from life to progress to the next step in spiritual development. Some people actually need harder experiences to grow the fastest. If you take those experiences away from them, they may still have to go through the experiences at some time in their development as Soul. The most expedient way to help people is to let them grow in their own way and in their own time. Neither you nor anyone else is graced with supreme wisdom to know what is best for another. This is why it is always best to give it to God.

Trusting and Surrender &

Trusting Spirit to guide your life is a fundamental lesson each Soul has to learn. Another name for trust with regards to Spirit is surrender. It is not an easy thing to explain or an easy concept to grasp. Trust sounds simple, but it evokes so many emotions from previous concepts that trusting is not easy to do or describe.

From my own life, I learned to trust only myself, until just recently. As I stated before, I was on my own at an early age and even when I lived at home, I still felt I had no one but myself to help me. It has been hard to allow others and (more importantly) Spirit into my life, to help and guide me. Since I've had to be my own strength in the past, I have felt vulnerable if I asked for help or relied on or trusted someone else to help me. Consequently, I have had a very hard time with trusting or surrendering my will and the direction of my life to Spirit.

Another reason I had a hard time with surrendering is because I encountered people who said, "God is doing this for them." Then they relinquished responsibility for their lives and lived as victims, thinking God is going to do their work for them. I am emphatically against this! I have grown because I accept responsibility for my life, and I am not about to give this up and be a victim. Being responsible for my life has given me a feeling of control and power over my life which I never before experienced.

So how do you take responsibility for your life and surrender and trust Spirit at the same time? Trust is formed step by step. It does not happen overnight. Remember Cause and Effect: the more actions you make to connect with Spirit and let Spirit guide your life, the more you will find Spirit guiding your life. This happens in conjunction with the responsibility you take in your life. This is the marked difference. The two ideas miss if they are taken separately. You can't effectively live your life if you live it as a child waiting for God to change your life without any action from yourself, or living from will-power alone. Surrender is a marriage of self-responsibility and uniting with Spirit. You have to make all the actions you possibly can and, at the same time, ask for guidance of the highest order from God and Spirit. Surrender is a balancing of strong self-responsibility and hearing and accepting Spirit's guidance in your life.

The more your actions are based on trust, the more trust you will develop. Some individuals have more to learn about the responsibility side of this process, while others have to ease into the trusting, guiding part. Know, like everything else in life, it is a process. Because of all my years of doing things for myself and being responsible, it felt strange at first to let Spirit into my life, to trust what was happening was for my growth and higher development. But the more I surrender my will and ego to Spirit while taking responsible actions for my growth, the happier my life becomes and the more I feel the presence of God in my life.

In surrendering, I am not negating my responsibilities of my growth to someone else or even to God. I am working in **partnership** with the higher aspect of all life, which is Spirit. I am learning Spirit promotes my good and abundance through my mind, body, emotions, and Soul. Even if I experience something I'd prefer not to, I am learning it is the easiest and fastest route to my happiness. When I used my will alone, situations would manifest in my life that were far from easy and good, and my life was much more of a struggle.

Partnership with Spirit ❧

How do you know when you are in partnership with Spirit? It is like trying to answer, "What does falling in love feel like?" The usual answer is that you know it when you experience it. The two examples are very similar. You will know when you are in partnership with Spirit. It is beyond logic and reason.

I know when I come from my ego, I am more tense and I do not feel as loving or tuned into life. When I come from my heart during my contemplations and dedicate my actions as a vehicle to Spirit, my whole day has a different feeling. I feel more relaxed about everything and more protected. I have more inner peace. I still do all the things I want and need to do to live on this planet but, because of this partnership and dedication to Spirit, the actions I take, from work to play and everything in between, become filled with purpose. No longer is my life a series of empty actions to accomplish or to fill up time. The whole of my life is transformed to something profound. Nothing in your life from the time you dedicate your actions and self to Spirit is inconsequential. Your whole life becomes filled with purpose. You will KNOW you are working with Spirit.

In this process of surrendering my life to Spirit, I make responsible decisions but I feel less alone. Before, I felt like it was me against the world. Now, slowly, I feel the world and I are partners. I feel I am protected, always. It's similar to studying a martial art with a wonderful master teacher. With the teacher you learn more quickly and effectively, with less damage to your body because the master is guiding you. Without the master you could still learn, but it could take longer and your injuries might be more severe. We all have the freedom to choose. You can go your whole life alone or you can choose to have help. As with the master martial arts instructor, the teacher does not do the work for you. He or she is there to guide you and make your progress faster and easier.

Faith ❧

Another important value to help you live life more deeply is faith. One aspect of faith is realizing something is true. It is formed by the proof of your experience, not because someone has told you it is true. Faith is also a process, as are trust and surrender. Faith can start as an inkling that a concept might be true. Then, with testing and experience, your faith can grow.

Faith is not something that can be pushed on you. It is developed through your inner knowing. No matter what anyone teaches, don't have faith in it until it rings true for you. If you have faith in something just because an authority tells you to believe, you take responsibility away from yourself. True faith is knowing in your heart that something is true for you, and it is the freedom to decide to hold on to or let go of what is true for you. Faith is an evolution. No matter what, faith is not a passive state. Living your life with faith is dynamic and action-oriented! Let it unfold for you!

Having faith is different from relinquishing responsibility and power within yourself. You need to always discern whether any teaching is right for you. Most people equate faith as giving up personal power, but having faith is empowering, because faith is an inner knowing no one can take away. Develop faith because of your own understandings, not because a minister, teacher, or anyone else has told you what to believe.

Similarly, if someone always treats you with respect and love, your knowing and experience of the friendship and your faith in the person is real. No matter what anyone tells you, you have your own experience. No one can convince you otherwise. Your faith in your friendship was developed by actions taken by both of you. You did not develop faith because someone told you to believe in the person. You have faith in that relationship because of your experience of it.

Faith As an Inner Awareness ❧

Faith also can start as an inner awareness that something can be done or achieved, and this awareness can be nurtured by your actions and the proof you encounter. It's similar to wanting to learn something new. First, you have the idea that you can learn or do a particular thing. As you continue with this new endeavor, your faith in yourself and your skill grows.

With faith you can achieve tremendous things in your life. The more conviction you have, the faster your life changes. A great way to increase your faith is to cultivate the attitude of be, do, and then have. The most powerful way to create things and change in your life is to first **be** the person inwardly you need to be. Then make all the actions needed (**do**), and you will achieve the proper results (**have**).

For example, suppose you want more money in your life. You have to first examine your beliefs. In my own life, I found out that I wanted money and financial independence because I felt it would give me more security. As I continue to grow in awareness I realized I have to achieve

233

that security within myself first, before changes can occur in my outer environment. Nothing on the outside of your life can change without changing your inner self first. When you change your inner self, that energy shift will change your outer environment.

Because what I truly desired was security, I have been concentrating on making my inner self feel more secure and safe, with or without money. This point is important! You need to be the way you want to be in your inner self first, even if your don't have the things you want on the outer part of your life, before these results manifest physically.

The formula for you making more money might be like this: First feel with the inner core of yourself that you do have the things you want already. Next, with the outer part of your life take all the appropriate actions to change your financial picture. Set goals, visualize results, work at the things you need to receive the money. Next, release your desire with faith to Spirit. Every time I follow this formula for change I create what I want, and it's done in the most efficient way I can imagine. At the same time, I am growing from my highest self, because I have released the attachments to specific outcomes. The more I let Spirit guide me, the happier I become.

Appreciation ❧

Part of "be" encompasses appreciation of what's in your life right now. Appreciation is an attitude of abundance, whether you have the thing(s) in your life you want or not. The more you express appreciation and **feel** it in your heart, the more will be manifested for you in your life.

The state of appreciation is so powerful I can't emphasize it enough! The more you focus on appreciating what's in your life now, the more you are setting up causes that emphasize abundance. Just feeling thankful is an action of acknowledgement to life. The acknowledgement is for what is in your life right **now**. Most people complain

234

and emphasize with their thoughts or words about what they don't have. When they do this, they focus on the lack instead of the abundance. Remember, what you focus on you attract to you. When you focus on appreciation, you focus on your abundance instead of lack. With appreciation, you set the stage in your life to receive even more! You create actions that manifest abundance.

When your heart is filled with appreciation, you open your heart up for more love and more Spirit. Your energy becomes more relaxed and, in this relaxed state, you contact Spirit. When you are tense you tend to shut down your flow with Spirit, which shuts down your power to create and receive.

Blessing a Situation ❧

Another attitude to help you see things from a broader perspective comes from blessing any situation that is hard to handle. Say to yourself, "I am blessing this situation in the name of God," or "May the blessings be." You are not trying to control any feelings or people. You are raising your vibrations and with this action you release control over any particular outcome. You are asking to be led to a higher way of interacting with the particular situation. This helps you to be free of the pull of any lower energy that your mind or ego might want to create or any negative energy that might be coming from someone else.

Suppose, for instance, there is someone you see frequently whose physical appearance or personality turns you off. It might be easy to put the person down or feel disgusted. Neither action raises your consciousness to a higher level. To keep yourself from lowering your vibrations and putting negative energy toward another, you can say to yourself, "May the blessings be," or "In the name of God." You are NOT trying to change the other person. You are blessing the situation to raise your thought processes and vibrations, so you can be above any negative mental

235

or emotional causes. Whenever you are linked with Spirit, fear and pettiness leave you and once again love and Spirit flow through your life.

In my own life, I find myself silently blessing a situation when I am at a point where I need to get above my negativity or worry. It helps calm me down and raises my consciousness in the process. It helps my human mind to remember why I am here.

Remember, the whole point of this book is to help you realize Spiritual principles are not separate from your life. Lovingly use these guides with yourself. The more you integrate Spirit into your life, the more your physical life manifests this change. A spiritual integration of life is not an intellectual understanding or an esthetic practice. Spiritual integration is a vibrant, whole life. Every level of your existence, from Soul to your physical body, is positively affected by your using these laws and the love of Spirit.

Spirituality is not just for when you die, it is for your life right now! There is only now. Wherever you go, even in death, there is only now. So wherever you find yourself, use the moment that you have to grow to your fullest. Spiritual growth is never separate from where you find yourself in the moment. If you separate your spiritual life from your daily life or wait until you die to understand life, then you are missing your chance for growth.

Live life with all the zest and joy and multitudes of experiences you desire. You are Soul. Soul is here to learn, and you learn from doing. Be, do, and have! Let Spirit guide your learning. Boundless joy and awareness are waiting for you. By your awakening, live ALL that is here for you NOW !

MAY THE BLESSINGS BE !

Marian Massie continues to research the outcomes and effects of the teachings in this book. Please send personal growth stories or accounts of your experiences that are the results of using these teachings! She is also available for lectures, seminars, personal appearances, and private counseling.

To contact her, please write or phone:

Advanced Perceptions, Inc.

1820 Water Place • Suite 150
Atlanta GA 30339
(404) 956-0554

Order Form

To order copies of this book, please use this form.
No book orders by phone, please.

Make checks (U.S. funds only) payable to Advanced Perceptions (at the address above), including a shipping and handling charge of $3.50 for the first book and $1.50 for each additional copy.

# Copies	X	Cost	=	Subtotal	+	Shipping	=	Total
_____		@ $11.95 each		_____		_____		_____

Please charge this order to my ❏ Visa ❏ Mastercard

Card Number_____

Signature _____ Exp_____

Name _____ Phone (____)_____

MailingAddress _____

City_____ State _____ Zip_____

Mail to: Advanced Perceptions,
   1820 Water Place, Suite 150, Atlanta GA 30339

Glossary

AFFIRMATIONS
Statements, either written or repeated to yourself in a positive, present-tense way, that facilitate acceptance of new goals or beliefs at the conscious and unconscious levels.

ASTRAL UNIVERSE
The next highest universe after the physical universe.

AT CAUSE
Being in union with the positive in life. You are the initiator, not the victim.

ATTACHMENT
To have your energy fixed or joined to something or someone in a way that causes mental, emotional, or physical pain if you no longer have it, him, or her in your life.

BELIEFS
Thought patterns used by your mind to communicate to yourself and others in this physical universe.

CAUSAL UNIVERSE
The next highest universe after the astral universe.

CONSCIOUS MIND
The seat of reason and logic where we are aware (conscious) of the thoughts held here.

CONTEMPLATION
An active tool you can use in the physical body to connect to God or Spirit; a spiritual exercise.

CULTURAL PROGRAMMING
Society's beliefs or perceptions about what is real or right.

DEFENDING BOUNDARIES
Protecting yourself from someone else's aggression; defending your right to be your own person.

DETACHMENT
A state of awareness that whatever is happening in your life is perfect for your growth. It is a letting go of your internal ego or emotional struggle as to how things have to be.

DIVINE LOVE
Giving love from a place in Soul which is in union with Spirit and God.

DREAMS
Ways in which we learn and communicate to ourselves and a way Spirit teaches or communicates to us.

DUALITY
Opposites, a two–fold distinction.

DYSFUNCTIONAL FAMILIES
Families where children haven't gotten the message that they are loved unconditionally.

DYSFUNCTIONAL NURTURER
A person who takes responsibility for other people's feelings, responses, or needs in a consistent, chronic way that is detrimental to the growth of either person.

EFFECT
Result.

EMOTIONAL BALANCE
The state of an individual with self-esteem and sense of self-worth who is not afraid to feel what he or she needs to feel.

ETHERIC UNIVERSE

The last universe that has any kind of form; the last universe before you experience yourself as total Soul.

ETHICS

The study of standards of conduct and moral judgment of a particular person, religion, group, or profession.

FEAR

Emotional response to perceived or real danger; a restrictive energy.

FORGIVENESS

A point in one's consciousness where one realizes no one is to blame for anything.

GOD-REALIZATION

An elevated state of consciousness or awareness; a direct knowing and communion with God and Spirit in the human form.

GUILT

A feeling you have done something wrong; a form of self–punishment.

HARMONY

Peaceful balance or order.

HEALTHY SELF

Someone who consistently makes loving actions in life to be whole; someone who can love him or herself for being, not for accomplishments.

KARMA

Accumulated effects from previous actions, from this life or past lives. Karma can be positive or negative.

LAW OF CAUSE AND EFFECT
Universal spiritual law that states whatever action you take in life has result(s) because of that action.

LAW OF NON-INTERFERENCE
A spiritual law of letting go of control of other people.

MARTYR
Person who does not take responsibility for life; person who never accepts self-love fully.

MASS CONSCIOUSNESS BELIEF
The collective beliefs of a group of people, or all the people on this planet, at any given time; shared reality.

MENTAL UNIVERSE
The universe between the causal and etheric universes.

MIND
The physical tool Soul uses to think with and communicate ideas and knowledge, composed of the conscious and subconscious mind.

NON-JUDGMENT
A letting go of how something or someone "should" be.

PHYSICAL BODY
The flesh and bones that make up a human being.

PHYSICAL UNIVERSE
The universe that is densest in form, the one we live in as human beings.

POLARITY
The condition of being positive or negative with respect to some reference point; having of two contrary qualities.

REINCARNATION
One's Soul being reborn into the appropriate place of existence to learn the lessons it needs in order to grow in itsawareness of God.

ROMANTIC LOVE
Love which is idealized, usually limited to sexual or emotional exchange in a relationship.

SELF–SABOTAGE
Unconscious detrimental actions to one's happiness and growth.

SHAME
The unconscious feeling one is worthless or a mistake.

SICKNESS
State of unbalance in the physical body, caused by emotional, mental, physical, or spiritual reasons.

SOUL
An individual Spirit composed of the sound and light of God; a happy, joyous, loving entity who is at peace.

SPIRIT
All that is emitted from God: light, sound, love; the forming substance of life.

SPIRITUAL PRACTICE
A tool one uses consistently to connect to higher self and Spirit.

SURRENDER
Trust in Spirit.

THOUGHTS
Energy waves that create.

VALUE

Worth in life; the things one needs to do for total growth and unfoldment as Soul.

VIBRATIONS

Energy waves; the movement of the light and sound.

VICTIM

Someone who doesn't allow personal needs to be met.

WAKING DREAM(S)

Hidden message(s) in average daily occurrences.